Equipping your Church to minister to Ex-Offenders

EQUIPPING YOUR CHURCH TO MINISTER TO EX-OFFENDERS

Louis N Jones

CONQUEST BOOKS

Washington, D.C.

Conquest Books
A division of ConquestHouse, Inc.
PO Box 73873
Washington, DC 20056-3873

Copyright 1998, 1999, 2000 ConquestHouse, Inc. All rights reserved.

Printed in the United States of America

ISBN: 0-9656625-0-0

Scripture quotations ending with the abbreviation (NASB) taken from the New American Standard Bible, copyrighted 1960, 1962, 1963, 1968, 1971, 1972, 1973, 1975, 1977, by the Lockman Foundation. Used by permission.

Scripture quotations ending with the abbreviation (NIV) excerpted from *Compton's Interactive Bible NIV*. Copyright (c) 1994, 1995, 1996 SoftKey Multimedia Inc. All Rights Reserved

TABLE OF CONTENTS

PREFACE VII

CHAPTER ONE 1
THE EX-OFFENDER MINISTRY: NEEDS AND GOALS 1
    THE NEED 1
WHO ARE EX-OFFENDERS, AND WHY SHOULD THE CHURCH REACH OUT TO THEM? 2
    WHY IS IT SO DIFFICULT TO GET THE CHURCH INVOLVED? 3
    THE GOAL OF EX-OFFENDER MINISTRY 6

CHAPTER TWO 9
PREPARATION AND OPERATION 9
    INITIAL PREPARATION FOR THE EX-OFFENDER MINISTRY 9
    MAKE SURE THIS IS GOD'S WILL FOR YOU 9
    GET THE BLESSING OF YOUR CHURCH LEADERSHIP 9
    GET CONGREGATION'S SUPPORT 10
    DETERMINE COMMUNITY ATTITUDES 10
    DEVELOP A MINISTRY TEAM 12
    VISIT OTHER POST-PRISON MINISTRIES 13
    PREPARE FOR THE NEEDS OF THE EX-OFFENDER 14
        Immediate Needs 14
        Secondary Needs 17

CHAPTER THREE 23
OTHER ISSUES REGARDING THE EX-OFFENDER MINISTRY 23
    DEPEND ON THE LEADING OF THE HOLY SPIRIT 23
    Find out all you can about the ex-offender 25
    Let the ex-offender know what is expected of him before joining 26
    Dealing with racial issues AND OTHER CULTURES 26
    FINANCING THE EX-OFFENDER MINISTRY 27
        Maintain your relationship with the Lord through faith 28
        Start out with what you have been given 28
        Research potential financial prospects 29
        Maintain relationships and cultivate these prospects 31
        Manage the money well 31
        Stick with it 32
    PEDOPHILES AND SEX OFFENDERS 33
        Megan's Law: 33
        Kansas Sexual Predator Law 33

CHAPTER FOUR 37
LOVE, DISCIPLESHIP, AND MINISTRY 37
    GODLY LOVE TOWARD THE EX-OFFENDER-WHAT DOES IT MEAN? 37
    DISCIPLESHIP FOR THE EX-OFFENDER: Leaving the Nets 39
    Jesus Christ initiates the call to discipleship. 39
    Discipleship is to follow Jesus and His Word. 39
    Discipleship involves putting aside everything that could stand in the way of following Jesus. 40
    The goal of discipleship is to develop Christian character and to produce men and women who are equipped to disciple others. 42
    THE PRUNING PROCESS: HOW TO DEAL WITH SUFFERING 42

    THE SCRIPTURAL BASIS FOR THE MINISTRY TO INMATES AND EX-OFFENDERS 44
    SCRIPTURES RELATED TO PRISONERS 47

CHAPTER FIVE 53

  LEGAL AND ORGANIZATIONAL STRUCTURE OF YOUR MINISTRY 53
    GET THE LEGAL AND SPIRITUAL COVERING OF A LOCAL CHURCH 53
    LEGAL FORM OF YOUR ORGANIZATION 54

CHAPTER SIX 59

  STARTING AN AFTERCARE CENTER 59
    Getting Started 59

CHAPTER SEVEN 63

  THE HARVEST 63

APPENDIX 65

  OTHER RESOURCES 65
    Benefits for the Elderly and Disabled 65
    The Work Opportunity Tax Credit Act 66
    Federal and State bonding for ex-offenders 66
    International Union of Gospel Missions 66
    Teen Challenge 66
    Reentry Jail and Prison Ministry 67
    National Prison Ministries 67
  CONQUESTHOUSE TRANSITIONAL HOUSING FOR EX-OFFENDERS OPERATIONS MANUAL
  69

ENDNOTES 94

PREFACE

Churches have traditionally been sources of hope, healing, and wholeness for suffering populations all over the world. Throughout Church history there is a myriad of examples of churches and committed Christian individuals helping those in need. Long before the establishment of welfare and other forms of government support, the church has been active in helping to meet the spiritual and secular needs of those within the church walls and those outside of them. Even during the establishment of the modern day penal system, the church has never been far from involvement.

The problem is that the involvement of the church is mostly behind the walls of the prison. Quite a few churches have prison ministries that go inside of the prison to minister. Then, they come back out, and the men and women they minister to are still there. Moreover, this cycle repeats itself constantly. But what happens when the person gets out of prison? Can they come to our churches? Do we have mentors for them? Are there jobs awaiting them? The formerly incarcerated person has many issues to deal with upon release that, unfortunately, many churches are ill equipped to deal with. That is the reason for this manual.

Equipping Your Church to Minister to Ex-Offenders was developed by the staff of Conquest Offender Reintegration Ministries (CORM). We are a nonprofit post-prison ministry located in Washington, DC. We provide reintegration services to ex-offenders on their release from prison, and are supported by donations from churches, foundations, and individuals. This manual will give the body of Christ some practical suggestions on setting up post-prison ministries. It is our intent, in preparing this manual, to increase the pool of information available to the Church and to show the need to reach out to those released from prison.

The information in this guide is prepared based on our experiences in prison ministry, and is intended as general guidelines. It is not, however, a do-it-yourself manual. The ministry of working with formerly incarcerated men and women can be difficult and stressful work and is not something you should consider doing alone. Therefore, if you have had no experience in working with the formerly incarcerated, you may want to consult with your pastor or spiritual leader.

We pray that you are blessed by the reading of this guide, and that it helps you in your decision to begin a post-prison ministry. May God bless you.

CHAPTER ONE

The Ex-Offender Ministry: Needs and Goals

THE NEED

Conquest Offender Reintegration Ministries Board member Bobby Barnes knows first-hand what an ex-offender experiences on release for prison. Having spent 30 of his 64 years going in and out of prison, when he was finally released, it was a new and frightening experience for him. As he was quoted in an article written about himself, "I was scared to death when I was getting ready to be released. If you don't have a support group behind you, you're lost."

Other ex-offenders agree with Barnes and will report that one of the biggest causes of recidivism is "the abrupt transition back to society." According to an article published in a September 1994 edition of the Washington Post[1], the biggest problem that plagued those who were recently released was "fear, fear, fear."

These quotes provide a snapshot of the kinds of issues that ex-offenders face on release from prison. The ex-offender will often confront the pressures and prejudices of friends and family. He or she may have low self-esteem and feelings of failure, hopelessness, suspicion and apathy. Most ex-offenders leave prison with the same problems they had when they entered. Many have to face the same world they faced before they went into prison—a world where they see no choices other than crime, a world where it seems no one will care for them.

This is contributing to a high rate of rearrest across the country. Statistics from state governments place the recidivism rate at anywhere from 50 to 80 percent. The failure of the prison industry to rehabilitate inmates is well documented. Therefore, it is up to the church to go well beyond the scope of many government and secular programs and to develop faith-based solutions to the problem of recidivism. Many studies have showed that faith-based programs reduce recidivism among their participants.

WHO ARE EX-OFFENDERS, AND WHY SHOULD THE CHURCH REACH OUT TO THEM?

For the purposes of this manual, I will define "ex-offenders" as persons, juvenile or adult, who have broken a Federal, state, county or city ordinance, have been convicted and sent to jail or prison, have been released, and have determined that they will not break the law again. They are men and women with wives, husbands, children, aspirations, dreams, struggles and joys, and should be treated with dignity and respect. Many people would define an ex-offender as *anyone* who has been released from imprisonment. These people are better defined as *ex-prisoners*. The truth is that an ex-offender is someone who has put criminal offenses behind him and is prepared to begin a new life.

That might sound like a literal definition, but it is an important one for starting your ministry. Do you wish to begin an ex-offender ministry, or do you wish to begin an ex-prisoner ministry? The difference is that ex-offenders are people who have seen the error of their ways. Ex-prisoners may consist of people who have made up their minds to continue their criminal lifestyles. An ex-prisoner ministry is one dedicated to helping ex-prisoners become ex-offenders. Once they become ex-offenders, the ministry can then proceed to help them move into a crime-free lifestyle.

Hebrews 6:1-2 lists six foundation principles for living the Christian life. Before a Christian becomes mature, he must ground himself in these six principles. The first of these principles is *repentance from dead works*. Any ex-offender ministry must determine if its clients have truly repented of their past crimes. If repentance is not present, then you cannot move your clients into the support system that will be suggested in the rest of this book, because their lack of repentance, and their willingness to commit more crimes will only circumvent your best efforts. The ex-offender ministry is mostly concerned with helping the ex-offender live out his spiritual and natural life in accordance with his repentance.

This ministry is very important, not only because God desires that ex-offenders trust in Him, but because of the criminal justice statistics that reflect the high rate of recidivism in America. A study from the U.S. Department of Justice found that 62.5 percent of all released state prisoners are rearrested for a felony or serious misdemeanor within 3 years. Of those, 46.8 percent were convicted, and 41.4 percent returned to prison or jail. In some states, the recidivism rate is higher. For instance, in Washington, D.C., statistics from the D.C. Department of Corrections indicate that 55 percent of the released prisoners are rearrested. This suggests there is a tremendous need for churches and ministries to become involved in helping these men and women resist the lure of crime once they are released. But, sadly, the number of ministries working to help released prisoners, as opposed to those working with prisoners on the inside, is few. Many ex-offenders attest that many ministries come inside the prisons to minister, but few are waiting to help them when they get out.

A survey recently conducted by Conquest Offender Reintegration Ministries indicates that many people believe that ministry to ex-offenders is important. However, few of the respondents had a prison, ex-prisoner, or ex-offender ministry in their churches. The attitude of many Christians is "Yes, the ministry is very vital, but please don't do it in my backyard." Many are fearful of ex-offenders and ex-prisoners because of the possibility that they could relapse and commit another crime (this is especially true of sex-offenders and violent offenders). Others feel that criminal offenders should be punished for the rest of their lives (and many are, not because of a judicial sentence, but because of society's attitude toward them). Still others feel that many ex-prisoners and ex-offenders are con artists, cannot be trusted, are just waiting for the opportunity to take advantage of someone, and will even fake remorse to get in the good graces of church people. This stigma, fueled by politics and the media, creates a negative image of ex-offenders that fosters a reluctance to build ex-prisoner and ex-offender ministries.

So, given the attitudes and the foibles of ministering to ex-offenders, why bother?

Because many ex-offenders are poor, homeless, undereducated, products of broken homes, fatherless, abused, neglected, oppressed, depressed, greedy and abandoned. These factors made crime attractive to them, and these factors that make staying away from crime difficult, particularly when quick, easy money can come by robbing a bank, or selling drugs, or stealing a car or two. The Gospel of Jesus Christ calls the Church to respond to those who are downcast and afflicted, which includes ex-offenders.

WHY IS IT SO DIFFICULT TO GET THE CHURCH INVOLVED?

I wish I could say that every local congregation in our community that claims the name of Jesus Christ was beating down our door to sign up to mentor ex-offenders or to volunteer to help teach job readiness courses and Bible studies. Sadly, that is not the case. In fact, few have. Many Christians are not embracing the vision of helping ex-offenders get on their feet (unless it involves money). There are not many congregations of any denomination willing to take up the cause of keeping ex-offenders out of prison.

As I mentioned above, much of it is fear. The scourge of crime around our nation has kept many people locked in their homes, afraid to venture out either night or day. The media's non-stop coverage of criminal acts has caused people to be suspicious even of their next door neighbors. Because some people (even those in the church) are wary and doubtful of God's ability to change people, an ex-offender to them represents a crime waiting to happen. Their only concern is to keep themselves and their loved ones out of harm's way, and to avoid taking chances on anything or anyone that could prove dangerous.

But it is not just fear. Ex-offender ministry presents some unique challenges to the church—challenges the church is unwilling to meet. In illustrating my statement, I present to you to the table below, drawing a correlation between prison/ex-offender ministry and a ministry that has been widely embraced by the church, children and youth ministry. Both ministries are called for in the Bible, and both are tremendously important, but the church has seen fit to embrace children and youth more than ex-offenders. In fact, there is hardly a Christian church over 30 members that does not have some specialized ministry or outreach to children. Far more lacking are churches that have raised up post-prison ministries.

In this table, I have presented ideas why the children's ministry is so popular, compared with ideas why the ex-offender ministry is so unpopular.

Figure 1

CHILDREN/YOUTH MINISTRY	PRISON/POST-PRISON MINISTRY
It is fairly easy to take authority over children and youth; they are more likely to respond according to our expectations	It is difficult, if not impossible, to take authority over some adult ex-offenders.
Children are teachable, and often do not challenge the teacher in areas of instruction.	Some adult ex-offenders can be difficult to teach; others are smart, know more about certain of instruction than many teachers, and can challenge the teacher or propose debate on certain subjects, particularly those about the Bible
Children are normally not physically imposing.	Some adult ex-offenders can be physically imposing.
Children are innocent and not responsible for everything they do because of their age.	Ex-offenders are perceived to be responsible adults, able to make decisions that would have kept them out of a life of crime. They are perceived to have deserved their time in prison.
Just about every church and community has children.	Not many churches or communities have known ex-offenders.
Children are cute, sweet and playful, naturally giving and drawing compassion and affection.	Ex-offenders can be hardened and tough from being in the streets; it can be difficult for them to give or draw compassion or affection.

In general cases, children's ministry may not involve caring for the whole needs of the child, such as shelter, clothing, food, health care, schooling, and spiritual nourishment.	Ministry to ex-offenders often involves all the mentioned items and others such as job training, job location assistance, life skills, etc.
Children are helpless, unable to care for themselves, and have to depend on adults for their every need. This makes them subservient to adults, and thus easier to manage.	An ex-offender may not feel subservient to anyone, even though he may be dependent on an adult for assistance. Since they are adults with their own will and the ability to fulfill it, they are much more difficult to manage.
Children are seldom responsible for crimes against the person, and are thus unlikely to cause anger and bitterness.	There are many people who are angry and bitter because of having been crime victims. This anger and bitterness can turn into revenge and will likely manifest itself against the individual perpetrator, or against all former and current lawbreakers.
Children usually have a set pattern. They wake up at a certain time of day; they go home and go to sleep at a particular time of night. Children's ministry is often relegated to a set time or hour.	Adult ex-offenders come and go as they please—they make their own decisions and keep their own schedules. An ex-offender minister may have to wake up in the middle of the night to tend to an issue about an ex-offender.

To sum this chart up, children's ministry is easy to put into the daily schedule of the average person without much of a disruption of his routine lifestyle. Children's ministries can often be organized in churches with little risk or potential for repercussion that could occur in an ex-offender ministry. On the other hand, ex-offender ministry involves time, money, and dedicated and committed Christians. It often breaks the boundaries of our comfort zones and causes us to involve ourselves heart, mind, body and soul to restoring an ex-offender.

It has been suggested to me that Satan is especially working overtime on ex-offender ministry because it is such a vital ministry. I agree that ex-offender ministry is vital. But to suggest that Satan has concentrated himself partially or exclusively on ex-offender ministry is absurd. In fact, the enemy attacks children's ministry just as much as he attacks ex-offender ministry. He attacks the music ministry just as much as he attacks the ministry from the pulpit. Satan hates anything and anyone that righteously represents the name of Jesus. He hates anything and anyone that will endeavor to snatch souls out of his hands and return them to Jesus. The ex-offender ministry is under attack, as are other ministries. But the ex-offender ministry brings us out of our comfort zones, to a place where, unfortunately, many Christians are too selfish or too lazy to go.

THE GOAL OF EX-OFFENDER MINISTRY

The goal of ex-offender ministry should be well beyond what can be achieved through human effort. If the goals you set for your ministry are merely to keep your charges out of prison, or to get them a job, then your goals are not lofty enough. The fact is, any secular or government organization can get someone a job. But only the power of God can change the hearts of men and women. As ex-offender ministers, you are agents and facilitators through which flow the power and blessings of God. Therefore, our goals as prison and ex-offender ministers should be no different from the goals the Lord has for His people. Consider Ephesians 4:17-24:

17So I tell you this, and insist on it in the Lord, that you must no longer live as the Gentiles do, in the futility of their thinking. 18They are darkened in their understanding and separated from the life of God because of the ignorance that is in them due to the hardening of their hearts. 19Having lost all sensitivity, they have given themselves over to sensuality so as to indulge in every kind of impurity, with a continual lust for more. 20You, however, did not come to know Christ that way. 21Surely you heard of him and were taught in him in accordance with the truth that is in Jesus. 22You were taught, with regard to your former way of life, to put off your old self, which is being corrupted by its deceitful desires; 23to be made new in the attitude of your minds; 24and to put on the new self, created to be like God in true righteousness and holiness (NIV).

This Scripture, written by Paul the Apostle from a prison cell, gives an outline of the goal for any prison ministry, which is as follows:

1) to introduce the ex-offender to Jesus and to teach him in accordance with the truth of the gospel, leading him to repentance and rejection of his former ways;
2) to establish an intimate, obedient relationship between the ex-offender and Christ through the preaching and teaching of the Word of God, so that the ex-offender is mentally and spiritually fed and reflects the righteousness and holiness of Christ.

These goals are meant to ensure the ministry doesn't become just a "social service organization", but is working to change lives both on the inside and the outside. Spiritual and mental maturity is the base on which any social service function should remain. In fact, studies have shown that prisoners who take part in spiritual exercises such as Bible studies have a lower rate of recidivism than those that do not.

CHAPTER TWO

Preparation and Operation

INITIAL PREPARATION FOR THE EX-OFFENDER MINISTRY.

MAKE SURE THIS IS GOD'S WILL FOR YOU

I will assume at this point that you have prayed to God and he has given you a burden for ministering to ex-offenders. If this is not the case, then I would suggest, before reading the rest of his pamphlet, that you pray and ask God if this is His will for you at this time. Ministry to ex-offenders will involve much time and effort. Some, *but not all*, of the ex-offenders you serve may have hidden motives, and want nothing more than to take advantage of you. Some, *but not all*, will con you to make you think they are serious about the Lord, when they are not. Others, *but not all*, will be doing so well, and then suddenly relapse. It takes a person and a church of great spiritual fortitude to handle a ministry to ex-offenders. Yet, when an ex-offender ministry is properly prepared, and its servants are prayed-up Christians who are committed to the ministry, then it will yield a great many fruits. To this day, many ex-offenders are accepting the salvation of Jesus Christ and are moving on to become mighty men and women or God. Some have become teachers, lawyers, doctors, preachers, and pastors. Other have blossomed into counselors, artists, musicians, and hard-working laborers. The harvest that is awaiting in the nation's prisons require laborers who are willing to go that extra mile to ensure that what inmates have received inside, does not evaporate outside.

GET THE BLESSING OF YOUR CHURCH LEADERSHIP

Before beginning this ministry, I would strongly recommend that you consult with your church leadership and ask their support. Remember, if God gave you the burden for this ministry, He will give you the tools to perform it. If your church leadership does not support the idea of an ex-offender ministry in your church, then I would strongly recommend that you honor your church leadership (Hebrews 13:17, Titus 3:1-2). Often God gives us burdens for ministry and shows us the vision, but others have not yet caught on to that vision. Perhaps you need to be prepared further, and perhaps they do, but it does no one any good to dishonor the edict of the church leadership. *This does not mean that you should let the vision die!* Continue to pray and seek God's direction, and trust that the Holy Spirit will reveal to you the direction that you must take. If you are certain that God has called you to start an ex-offender ministry, then it would be wise to ask God where and when to begin. Perhaps you could start a ministry outside your church, or join with others who are ministering to ex-offenders. Some churches will not support the idea of the ministry being based in their churches, but will support the idea of you taking part in another ministry.

GET CONGREGATION'S SUPPORT

If your church leadership is supportive, then you need to go to the congregation. Schedule a meeting with your church membership to present to them the idea of starting an ex-offender ministry. Give them Scriptures and teaching to show God's attitude toward prisoners and ex-offenders (see *Scriptures Related to Prisoners*, toward the end of this manual). Remember that it is the church membership that will interact with the ex-offenders daily, so you need to get their input and their support. Many prison ministers have invited ex-offenders to the church, only to discover the people of the church have a hostile or fearful attitude toward ex-offenders. The ex-offender may feel uncomfortable there and will not want to return, which may affect his opinion and outlook about Christians in general. Also, many church members may feel uncomfortable with the idea of ex-offenders sitting next to them in church, and will not return. However, if you have the backing of the church leadership and there are enough people in the congregation who are ready to support you (with time or money), you have enough to take the next step in starting the ex-offender ministry.

DETERMINE COMMUNITY ATTITUDES

As well as getting the support of your church congregation and leadership, you need to determine if it is feasible to operate the ministry in your community. This is particularly true if you will start a residential ministry (see *Starting An Aftercare Center*, later in this manual). The following story is a good example of why you should do this.

A few years ago in the community in Washington, DC where I live, a local ministry purchased a multi-unit apartment building that had been vacant and boarded up for many years. They obtained a building permit and began renovation. Shortly after they began, they called a community meeting which was held at our church, directly across the street from the apartment building. Our little church normally holds only 75 people, but 90 people managed to pack the church building for this meeting. People in the audience included the neighborhood Advisory Neighborhood Commissioner, who is an unpaid elected government official responsible for serving as a liaison between the citizens and the city government, the area City Councilwoman Charlene Drew Jarvis, representatives from a neighborhood civic association, and the pastor from another nearby church.

The president of the ministry, a thin, unassuming man, stood up before the crowd, introduced himself, and told them about the organization that had bought the building. The crowd was silent at this point as they listened intently. However, the tone changed markedly when the president started to explain their intent for the building.

He told the crowd that the building would be used to provide transitional housing for men and women who had been struggling with drug addiction and homelessness. Immediately some in the crowd began whispering to each other. However, things didn't get out of hand until it was time for the audience to ask questions.

"Why don't you place this facility in the neighborhood where you live?" asked a woman who lived in the neighboring suburbs of Maryland.

"Why are you putting a drug treatment facility in our neighborhood?" asked another. (It was not a drug treatment facility, but a housing arrangement for former addicts who were clean and regularly and gainfully employed.)

"We already have a facility like this in our neighborhood!" someone else shouted, referring to a youth rehabilitation home directly across the street from the building.

"This is an illegal facility," someone else mentioned. (She falsely determined the facility's official designation as a rooming and boarding house was incorrect based on her suspicion that drug treatment would be going on in the facility.)

Even though the meeting was intended to tell the community of the plans for the building, the residents did not like the plans. Many refused to accept the fact that the building would be a drug-free transitional housing center, but classified it as a drug treatment center, which would have required neighborhood approval to receive an occupancy permit. The meeting ended with many people angry and intending to stop the progress on the building.

The next day, rocks were thrown at the building, smashing its new windows. A few days later, there was an organized protest outside the building, which drew the media's attention to the case. The civic association filed suit to have the ministry stop construction until it gained a building permit that would approve construction of a drug treatment facility. The efforts succeeded in stopping any further construction until the issues were sorted out in court.

A few weeks later, the court decided. The court found that the neighborhood association had no right to hinder the organization from doing its work. The ministry was given the go-ahead to finish construction. Praise the Lord!

After construction started again, more windows were broken out. This time, the ministry left the windows broken and continued to fix up other areas of the building. When construction was just about completed several months later, the community's defeat had set it, and community anger over the project had subsided.

Today, that building is one of the best-managed and neatest buildings on the block. The programs have been running there for several years now, and there has never been a problem in the community resulting from this building. The people that come in and out of the building you would never believe were former addicts unless you asked them. God was victorious over this situation.

The community can hinder your ministry just as effectively as the church can. But it does no good to ignore the issue. Set up meetings with the key people in the community where you desire to operate this ministry, particularly if you are going to operate a residential outreach. Tell them about your ministry and the good that it will do. They may still oppose your vision, but at least you know what to expect before beginning. The ministry that operated the transitional housing center in my community was caught off guard by the community's reaction, and was unprepared for the community backlash they received. Talking about your project with the key leaders in the community will give you a sense of what the community view and attitude is about your ministry, and you will know how to deal with it. Perhaps if the environment is too hostile, you may consider going elsewhere.

But don't stop there. Talk also with the residents of the community (you'd be surprised at how leaders can be out of touch sometimes). Find out what their feelings are about such an outreach. All of this research will give you information that you need to either put together a strategy for achieving your ministry goals, or to plan to locate your outreach elsewhere. It will give you feedback to find out if it is feasible to operate an ex-offender ministry in your community.

This process has the secondary benefit of making the community feel that they were important and vital enough to your project to have been asked their thoughts. That alone can soften people's attitudes toward your outreach. The community may not like what you are doing, but they will like it even less if you try to sneak it in behind their backs. Unless you plan to hide your ministry, it is best if the community knows about it before any work is done. You may also assuage negative attitudes and fears by giving responsible members of the community an opportunity to engage in the decision-making process of your ministry. Set up an advisory board consisting of community residents, and allow them to have input.

You may also want to structure your ministry in such a way that the positive benefit to the community far outweighs the negative views. For instance, a ministry in D.C. that works with ex-offenders and former drug addicts has a live-in program where the residents clean community streets, run errands for the sick and shut-in, shovel snow, and do minor repairs on some neighbor's homes.

DEVELOP A MINISTRY TEAM

Unless you plan to visit prisons alone, correspond with inmates alone, do research about inmates alone, be the lone person to invite them your church, be the only one to counsel and mentor them, and be the only one to do follow-up (neither of which I recommend), you will need a ministry team. A ministry team should consist of at least four committed, mature praying Christians who are stable, Spirit-filled, and who can give time and effort to the ministry. These people will do most of the ministry, but will also be involved with planning. (If you like, you can have both a ministry team, and a planning team.) Before you select a team, you should do a demographic study of the prisoners in your community and know the types of people that you will meet. This information will determine the makeup of your ministry team.

For instance, if most of the prisoners in your community are Spanish-speaking, then your ministry team will need to be comprised of ministers who are Spanish-speaking. If the prisoners are predominately male, then your ministry team needs to be predominantly male.[2] If your ministry will be geared to youth, then your team needs to be comprised of people who have a love for and a gift of relating to young people. If the ex-offenders you will serve include pedophiles, sexual abusers or violent offenders, your ministry team will need to be comprised of people trained to deal with these populations.

I would also recommend that your ministry team consist of at least one ex-offender who is proven and successful. The perspective of someone who has been there can be very valuable, both for the experience he brings to the program, as well as the testimony he provides to fellow ex-offenders. However, if you do not know any ex-offenders, then the advice of other post-prison programs (see below) can be very helpful.

Your ministry team should be responsible for training members of the church at how to deal with ex-offenders. Remember that some ex-offenders may enter the church looking for opportunities to con someone. They will look for the most gullible, inexperienced people, and those people probably will not be on your ministry team. Direct the members of your church that they are to check with the ministry team before making any commitments with the ex-offender, especially of money and time. Also, make sure the ex-offender knows that any requests should be directed through the ministry team. Dealing with ex-offenders involves a skillful mix or prudence and astuteness, mixed with Godly love and compassion.

VISIT OTHER POST-PRISON MINISTRIES

When I taste an excellent dish and I want to make it for me, I ask for the recipe. I don't try to recreate it, hoping I'll mix all the right ingredients and miraculously come up with the same taste. Interestingly enough, many people try for the hit-and-miss approach when it comes to developing ministries. I would recommend searching out those ministries that are already doing what you want to do, and taking your ministry team and visiting those ministries to learn, network and develop contacts. Perhaps the Lord has called you to join with those ministries instead of starting your own. In any event, the information you can get from these contacts can be very helpful.

When we started Conquest Offender Reintegration Ministries, one of the first things we did, and continue to do, was to attend meetings and outreaches of other ministries. In one instance, I took my entire Board of Directors and traveled to Pennsylvania to meet with the director of Liberty House, an aftercare ministry there. We told him on arriving that we were not there to pitch or sell our program. We were there to learn. The Pennsylvania ministry bought an old hotel in a small town and renovated it into a center to house several ex-offenders for 3 to 6 months. The program was very successful, and we wanted to emulate their success. While we were there, we took a tour of their transitional housing facility, met some of the residents, and talked with the director about how the program was organized. When we left, we had enough information to begin to plan our own aftercare outreach in Washington, D.C.

PREPARE FOR THE NEEDS OF THE EX-OFFENDER

When an inmate leaves prison and ventures into the outside world, he may have an immediate need for shelter, food, clothing, substance abuse treatment, fellowship, and spiritual guidance and mentoring. Other needs, which may not be as immediate, include employment, vocational training, literacy training, life skills training, and transportation. Your church must be prepared to either directly met these needs or be able to refer the ex-offender to people or agencies that are able to help.

As a young organization, your ministry may not have the finances, staff or facilities to directly meet all the needs listed below. Do not be tempted to do this. Your goal is not to establish a *super ministry*, able to directly meet every need your ex-offenders will ever have. It is imperative that you begin to establish partnerships with other service agencies in your community and to know what resources exist to meet the needs below.

In any event, all of these needs should be determined before the ex-offender leaves prison. It is not good to wait until the ex-offender is released before trying to figure out where he will stay or what clothes he will wear. Your ministry team should send a couple of people into the prison to visit with the inmate at least two months before his release and find out his needs.

Immediate Needs

SHELTER

Finding an ex-offender a good place to stay may be difficult. Many come out of prison with no place to go, no money, no other resources, and a prison record that would not appease many landlords. Before inviting ex-offenders to your church, particularly those about to be released from prison, you should make sure that you have adequate housing resources available. Perhaps someone in your church (or other churches) would be kind enough to allow the ex-offender a place to stay. Some communities have aftercare centers that will accept ex-offenders. Still others have organizations that can help with housing resources. Emergency shelters are a last resort, but only after all other methods have failed. Very often, emergency shelters have an environment that is not conducive to the ex-offender's development. One ex-offender recently told me that he went to a shelter immediately after leaving prison, only to find out that half the residents of the shelter were using drugs right there in the facility. It is important that the ex-offender finds a place to stay that is as far removed as possible from the influences that landed him in prison in the first place.

The problem here is that shelter, particular shelter that is worth anything, costs money. Few people are willing to let someone live with them rent-free. Of course, the ultimate approach would be to establish a transitional housing outreach of your own. But failing that, finding appropriate shelter for an ex-offender will take money. If your church has a budget for this, perhaps it can pay first and second month's rent on an apartment for an ex-offender, provided he moves on and gets a job. Another alternative would be getting the ex-offender a room at a rooming house. Perhaps someone in your church is willing to sponsor the ex-offender for a month or two until he finds gainful employment.

The shelter situation for many ex-offenders presents a Catch-22. For some, getting a job requires an address and a regular place to live (many employers require identification that lists the residence of the ID holder). Yet, getting an address and a regular place to live requires some income. Your job as a minister to ex-offenders requires that you help the ex-offender sort out these issues.

FOOD AND CLOTHING

Again, as with shelter resources, the ex-offender ministry must be able to help feed and clothe the people it serves.

For food, you might want to approach grocery stores or food banks in your community to ask for donations. It also may be a good idea to establish a food pantry of your own, stocked with donations from your church members or other people or businesses in the community. And you should make sure the ex-offender is invited to a sit-down meal with one of your team members at least once a week.

Th ex-offender should also have a satisfactory supply of clothing available when he or she leaves prison. Again, perhaps people in your church or businesses in the community would be willing to give clothing for a "clothing closet" that you could establish. Make sure that you have the inmate's clothing size before he or she leaves prison, and try to structure the ex-offender's wardrobe so a suitable variety of clothes is included. The ex-offender should have several changes of casual clothes, at least one pair each of dress shoes and casual shoes, and at least two sets of dress clothes.

MEDICAL TREATMENT

Your ministry must be prepared to either provide licensed medical services or refer your clients to licensed medical treatment facilities. The medical needs which your ex-offenders may have is varied. Female ex-offenders may be pregnant on leaving prison and will need immediate prenatal care. Some of your ex-offenders may be suffering with cancer, AIDS, physical injuries or other injuries. Make it a point to discover, before your ex-offender leaves prison, if he or she had any medical problems.

SUBSTANCE ABUSE TREATMENT

It will be important to determine if this need exists (in conjunction with other medical needs as stated above) before trying to assist with the other needs. If the ex-offender is abusing substances (just because inmates are locked up does not mean that they do not have access to illegal substances), then it is important that he receive treatment immediately. Develop a listing of Christian organizations in your area that provide treatment for substance abuse (two such organizations are Teen Challenge, and the International Union of Gospel Missions--see contact information for these ministries in the Appendix). Many churches are also running Christian programs based on 12 step principles. You may aid with other needs temporarily (such as food and clothing), but I recommend not embarking on any long-term plan of action until the substance abuse is treated.

The Lord can provide complete and total deliverance from drugs through the power of the Holy Spirit. I have seen men and women become complete free of drug addiction without the benefit of any methadone treatment. In fact, I share the opinion of some who believe that non-Christian approaches to drug treatment, including prescribing methadone, do not work long-term. Senator Spencer Abraham (R-Mich) in an interview with ReligionToday (www.goshen.net) said that while government funded drug treatment programs can be effective, in the long run they "have not made a dent in substance abuse" and that their methods have an "abysmal success rate."[3]

FELLOWSHIP

The Greek word for fellowship in the Bible is *koinonia*, which means *a sharing partnership*, a *communion*. The quality of your church's fellowship may determine whether the ex-offender wants to be a part of your congregation. Despite how *tough* they may seem, ex-offenders need love, encouragement, and acceptance just like everyone else. Since they have been stigmatized as unrepentant, irredeemable criminals by the world system, the only place where they can find the love, encouragement and acceptance they need (other than the streets) is in the church. An ex-offender church ministry must do everything possible to make ex-offenders feel as if they are a part of the fellowship and that they are loved and appreciated, whether they officially join the church or not.

SPIRITUAL GUIDANCE AND MENTORING

Spiritual guidance and mentoring remains one of the most important of the immediate needs. Ex-offenders often leave prison with low self-esteem, fear, and hopelessness. For instance, many ex-offenders will not look for a job because they feel they will never get one, or at least, never get one that will meet their needs. Many would rather sell drugs and rob banks than work a grueling 40-hour a week job for minimum wages. The attitudes and feelings that an ex-offender faces are issues that need to be dealt with if the church is to have any success at helping the ex-offender rehabilitate himself. Often ministries make the common mistake of helping the ex-offender get things such as a car, a house, and employment, believing that these things only will be effective, only to result in his getting fired and losing everything because he was too depressed to show up at work consistently. Meeting physical needs should be performing in conjunction with providing spiritual needs. One should not be sacrificed for the other.

Mentoring is an important part of this process. Mentors are responsible for providing support, encouragement and guidance to ex-offenders through trusted and wise Christian advisers who meet with them regularly to listen and to share knowledge and experience. Both mentors and participants should have input into deciding with whom they will be matched. *Mentor* is a Greek term meaning "adviser" or "wise man. A mentor can be a helpful source of information, encouragement, spiritual support, or just someone to talk to. Mentors should meet personally with ex-offenders at least once a month, help to meet the ex-offender's needs, and should always be available by phone. Many ex-offenders acknowledge they did better when they knew there was someone who cared about them.

An excellent manual, *Principles for Effective Mentoring of Ex-Prisoners*, is available through Prison Fellowship Ministries. To obtain this manual, write them at PO Box 1550, Merrifield, VA 22116-1550, or call 877-478-0100.

Secondary Needs

EMPLOYMENT OR VOCATIONAL TRAINING

You may be surprised that I placed this under Secondary Needs. After all, the prevailing wisdom among criminal justice circles is that getting a job should be one of the most important, if not *the* most important, things that an ex-offender should do. I am not diminishing the importance of getting a job-certainly it is important. But getting a job, as well as keeping a job, requires a certain level of responsibility and sensible conduct. Certainly you would not want to get a job for a guy who is struggling with substance abuse. And if the person has issues related to authority, proper conduct in the workplace, and is quick-tempered, any job he or he gets is likely to be lost within a few weeks.

Of course, the ex-offender's need for a job may preempt any other need, and there are some cases in which you have to meet whatever needs you can meet, and continue to work with the ex-offender to meet other needs. But my position here is that getting a job, while important, should never be judged as the *only* need. And when the immediate needs listed above can be met fairly quickly before the need for a job arises, I'd advise meeting them before sending the ex-offender off on a journey to look for employment. (For those who are unable to work, you should try to help them get some disability assistance through the Social Security Administration—more on this below).

Eventually, many of the ex-offenders in your ministry who are able to work will need to get a job. This may be a difficult undertaking, especially since many ex-offenders have no marketable skills, and others have not worked in years because of imprisonment. Your chief role in this will be to keep the ex-offenders encouraged to continue searching for employment despite the many obstacles they may face. You can help speed the process by:

- assessing skills obtained before, during and after prison

- Providing training in skills needed for gainful employment.

- arranging transportation to and from job interviews

- learning how to prepare resumes for ex-offenders

- teaching them how to conduct themselves on an interview

- finding low cost or free suits or dresses suitable for wearing to interviews

- contacting organizations skilled at helping ex-offenders find employment

- determining what legal papers are required for a job search and helping the ex-offender obtain them. Each ex-offender, before beginning a job search, should have a social security card, a birth certificate, a high school diploma or GED, and a DD214 for veterans of the Armed Forces. This information should be obtained before the inmate's release.

If the ex-offender has few marketable skills, vocational training may be an option. Vocational training can range from formal classroom training such as that found in many colleges and universities, to Old Uncle Pete giving a quick and dirty lesson in operating the backhoe. Though you may not want to opt for either extreme, there are plenty of opportunities available for those who wish to learn a marketable skill. Check with charitable organizations, churches, schools, and your city, county, state or Federal government for information on these opportunities, some of which are free and low-cost. Also, check around to see if someone in your church skilled with computers, or carpentry, or auto repair might be willing to offer a training course. If you church has the finances, sponsoring an ex-offender to attend a vocational course may be a possibility.

The goal here is not to just get the ex-offender a job and be done with it. The goal is to help the ex-offender *gain suitable employment that will enable him or her to care for self and family*. A $5.50 an hour job is okay to start with, but the salary, just above minimum wage, may not be enough. An inadequate job can sometimes be just as bad as no job at all.

TRANSPORTATION

Unless your church is located in an urban area where there are buses, taxicabs or subways available, the ex-offenders will need transportation to travel to and from church, work, and other places until they can find work and obtain their own transportation. Organize a corps of volunteers willing to drive ex-offenders to and from work, to the grocery store, and other essential places. If your church has a multi-passenger vehicle such as a bus or van, the bus could be used to pick up ex-offenders at certain times.

Be careful about giving an ex-offender a car to drive soon after he is released from prison (assuming he still has a valid driver's license). The only exception would be if the ex-offender needs a car to perform his job—if he was a pizza-delivery person, for example.

Often an ex-offender's rehabilitation depends on him NOT having access to certain places and certain areas. If he has a car and is free to go where he pleases, what's to stop him from going back to the people and places that got him in prison in the first place? Also, cars carry with them a financial responsibility that may be too difficult for ex-offenders just starting to get their lives together. Insurance, title, tags and maintenance, even on an old car, can easily run over $250 a month. Finding a place to live is a greater priority over finding a car.

LITERACY AND LIFE SKILLS TRAINING

Statistics from the U.S. Department of Education show that 19% of imprisoned adults are functionally illiterate (compared with 4% of all adult Americans), and 40% of imprisoned adults are completely illiterate (compared with 21% of all adult Americans). The rate of learning disabilities in adult correctional facilities is also high, at 11% (compared with 3% of all adult Americans). Therefore, the possibility of dealing with an ex-offender who cannot read or write well, if at all, is high. Any church or program dealing with ex-offenders must recognize this fact and be prepared to deal with it. I have heard of churches who bring illiterate ex-offenders into their congregations, give them Bibles and enroll them in Bible studies, not realizing the ex-offenders' inability to read the material. Churches should research educational programs in their community that provide literacy training and work with adults with learning disabilities. For spiritual education, Bibles on tape are excellent for individuals with below average reading skills.

REINTEGRATION WITH IMMEDIATE FAMILY

Many of your ex-offenders will have a spouse, parents or children on the outside. These relationships may be strained, if not dissolved altogether. One of the chief objectives of your ministry will be to help your ex-offenders become better people through the word of God so they can become better spouses, parents to their children, or children to their parents. This process will not take place overnight. Many ex-offenders have had little positive interaction with family and almost no relationship skills. Most married male offenders have to be taught how to be proper husbands. Most married female offenders have to taught how to be godly women. In addition, the issues of bitterness, anger, resentment, and jealousy usually pop up in relationships involving an ex-offender and other members of his or her family.

The role of your ministry, in addition to ministering the word of God to the ex-offender and his/her family, is to ensure that your ex-offender does not resume more responsibility in the family than he or she is ready for. Relationships, especially those that are strained, are often quite stressful, especially if there are children in the picture. Reintegration into the family should occur only after the ex-offender has had at least three months of solid discipleship and skills training and has developed a vibrant, active relationship with the Lord. He or she should know and be prepared to obey what the Bible has to say about family responsibilities. In the meantime, your ministry should help meet the needs of the family during this period, so the ex-offender can be free to concentrate on his own growth.

Do not be tempted to fudge on this requirement because of the "experience" of your ex-offender. He may be 50 years old, married for 21 years, and raised two children to adulthood. On the surface, he would seem to be an ideal candidate to reintegrate into the family immediately because of his "experience." Don't buy it. The saying, "age is nothing but a number" fits here. He can be 50 years old, but still acting and thinking like a 12-year old. His claim of raising two children doesn't mean that he currently has the strength and spiritual stamina to do it again. And because he has been married for 21 years does not mean it was a good marriage. I once knew a couple who was married for 30 years, but haven't slept in the same bed since their 10th anniversary!

Satan is crafty at using family to destroy ex-offenders. Again, the criteria should be, "Is he ready now?" Not "Has he done it before?" Is the ex-offender spiritually, physically and financially ready to resume his or her family responsibilities? Does he or she respond well to the teaching of the Word? Has the ex-offender been faithful to attend meetings? Does he or she act well under stress? Has the ex-offender been able to find and keep employment? Is the family supportive of the ex-offender's efforts to study the Word? Are there problems in the family, such as drug abuse or alcoholism, which could draw the ex-offender back into a life of crime? These and other questions should be answered before encouraging the ex-offender to return to his or her family.

This does not mean the ex-offender cannot have any interaction with his family. If the ex-offender has children, he or she should be allowed to see the children. The ministry should plan events for the ex-offender and the family to get together and interact regularly. But the ex-offender should not live with the family or assume a role as primary breadwinner unless he or she is ready for it.[4]

Be careful how you present this to the ex-offender, however. Never *command* that the ex-offender cannot see his or her family. In fact, never command an ex-offender to do *anything*. Communicate the fact that the ex-offender is free to do whatever he or she wants. But you should encourage the ex-offender to consider your assessment of his or her ability to handle the pressures of family. But if the ex-offender insists on reintegrating with his or her family, do not hinder it in any way. But make yourself available as a friend no matter what happens.

CHAPTER THREE

OTHER ISSUES REGARDING THE EX-OFFENDER MINISTRY

DEPEND ON THE LEADING OF THE HOLY SPIRIT

You need to understand, despite what many people will tell you, that entering the ministry to ex-offenders is entering a battle that will be fought on spiritual ground. Many of the ex-offenders you deal with will be under the influence of demonic spirits. Your primary and most important job as a minister will be to determine, through the Holy Spirit, what these demons are and to conduct spiritual warfare based on the word of God. Remember that the ministry to ex-offenders is not just a social service. You are fighting for the souls of men. The Scripture says in Mark 8:36, "For what does it profit a man to gain the whole world, and forfeit his soul?" (NASB). Unfortunately, there are many ministries that are doing exactly that. They are helping ex-offenders gain jobs, receive education, and get off welfare. These are all commendable goals that should be integrated into your ex-offender ministry. However, many of the clients of these ministries gain these things, but receive almost no training in the Word of God. They do not move on to establish a vital relationship with the Lord, chiefly because the ministry has not placed the ministry of the Word as a top priority. Do not make this mistake. The quality of your ministry is not predicated on how well you get ex-offenders jobs or educational opportunities, but on whether you use every opportunity to preach the Word.

This is especially important because of the obstacles that many ex-offenders will face. The temptations for an ex-offender to return to his or her previous lifestyle are overwhelming. In addition, employers will not be beating a path to the ex-offender's door to hire him. The taste of freedom for many ex-offenders is often so seductive that they will use that freedom to commit the same acts that landed them in prison in the first place. For ANY ex-offender to withstand these temptations, he needs a relationship with the Lord. He needs power from on high. Acts 1:8 proclaims that this power from on high is the Holy Spirit. The Holy Spirit is the one necessary element for ministry. He is your senior partner, without whom you cannot excel in this ministry.

The Holy Spirit is especially important in ministry because of two of the nine gifts of the Spirit found in I Corinthians 12. Those gifts are the *word of knowledge* and the *word of wisdom*. The word of knowledge is a fact revealed through the Holy Spirit and not through the efforts of the human mind. The word of wisdom is also supernaturally revealed, a word from God about how to apply knowledge received from revelation or through human training. Both of these gifts are indispensable in dealing with the demonic forces that compete for the hearts and souls of ex-offenders. Ex-offenders will enter your church with deep-seated problems that often have not been solved through imprisonment or even conversion to Christianity. These problems, if not detected, could manifest themselves in a way that is destructive or dangerous. For instance, if a pedophile joins a church, it would be unwise and dangerous to put him in a position where he would have unrestricted contact with children. As obvious as this seems, it happens every day in America. People come into churches with undetected and unchecked problems that have torn churches apart. It takes someone with Holy Spirit keenness to determine the types of influences prevalent in a person and to take a course of action.

So what role is served by clinical pyschologists, social workers, and other professional people who deal with the problems of men and women? These professions can only function from the knowledge learned about a patient through personal observation or through patient confession. These professions can be helpful in a ministry to ex-offenders, and their expertise should not be taken lightly and should be sought out. But the Holy Spirit, through a word of knowledge, can reveal things in a person they may not have had a chance to come to the surface through confession or other expression.

For instance, a gentleman not long ago joined our church after having left another church in the area. We did not know this man, but when he came to our church, he appeared the ultimate of Christian integrity—well dressed, a good job, a solid knowledge of Scriptures. He spoke in tongues, prophesied, and praised the Lord. To look at him on the surface, you would never have guessed that he was a child molester.

How did we know? One of our ministers received a word of knowledge from the Lord about it. Several other members of the congregation felt it in the Spirit. It was later confirmed by the pastor of the church from which the man had left; a pastor that was a good friend of our pastor and had noticed the man in the congregation during a special visit. But there was no way that a psychologist or psychiatrist could have known about the man's sin unless the man had showed it through his behavior or revealed it through his speech.

Psychologists and psychiatrists rely on learned knowledge obtained through the natural mind. But a supernaturally revealed word from the Holy Spirit is not dependent on natural knowledge. Even a child can receive a word from the Holy Spirit. I believe that was the case when a child from our congregation, who is normally affectionate and friendly, would not allow this man to touch him or hold him or even get near him. That child received a word from the Holy Spirit, a glorious and comforting indication that God protects his children, young and old.

You would do well to incorporate the gifts of the Spirit in your own ministry. I have only mentioned two here. But the other seven are also vital. This is not a Pentecostal teaching. This is Biblical truth that will add a depth and dimension to your ministry that is not achievable through natural effort.

FIND OUT ALL YOU CAN ABOUT THE EX-OFFENDER

Some prison ministries recommend that the ex-offender not be asked about the circumstances of his or her imprisonment. I do not entirely agree with this advice. If an ex-offender is to enter a church to be healed, it is *essential* that the ministry know the struggles he is having, so he can be dealt with properly. Even the doctor must know a patient's entire medical history before he can prescribe treatment for any complaints. Before a doctor prescribes penicillin for treating a disease, for example, he would need to know if the patient has any allergies to the medication. Failing to get this information beforehand could lead to him serious harming the patient, or even killing him. Similarly, failing to get an adequate history of ex-offenders could cause you to blindly prescribe spiritual therapies that could cause more harm than good.

Getting this information from ex-offenders need not be as direct as, "What were you in for?" types of questions. I would recommend that as part of normal counseling session, ask the ex-offender what types of struggles he has been having. This places the emphasis on the person, and not so much on the charge that a person had (which may be true or false). It also opens the potential for the ex-offender to discuss problems that may have nothing to do with his imprisonment. If he is honest, wants to be helped, and trusts you, he will also reveal the struggles that led him to prison. Make sure that the ex-offender knows that you are there as a representative of God, that you care for him, and that anything he says will not be unusual, strange or shocking.

Make sure that you are prepared for any answer the inmate or ex-offender may give you. Consider the most ugly, disgusting or wicked crime that you can think of. If the inmate or ex-offender told you he did such a thing, would you be able to handle it? Do not appear shocked or disgusted by the crime the inmate or ex-offender may have committed.

Also, be prepared for an answer that reveals little. Many ex-offenders will not readily share the intimate details of their lives with you until you have established trust.

If possible, also have the ministry team learn as much about the ex-offender as possible before he is released. Talk with his chaplains, his counselors, his caseworkers, and other prison ministers who have worked with him and get written referrals from them. (Note that these people may be expressly forbidden to give out any personal information unless the inmate has given written consent.) Go into the prison and talk with the inmate yourself. When the inmate has been released and comes to your church, he should have a relationship or a bond with someone there.

It is also important that when an inmate is released, to establish and maintain a relationship with his parole or probation officers.

LET THE EX-OFFENDER KNOW WHAT IS EXPECTED OF HIM BEFORE JOINING

Establish rules, and have a clear and concise vision and mission for your church and the ex-offender ministry. Everyone who comes into your ministry must know what is expected of him, what is *not* expected of him, and what goals the ministry has for each person who becomes a part. In love, communicate these things clearly before the ex-offender comes into your ministry. Establish a system for hearing grievances and dealing with complaints. Always keep the lines of communication open between the ex-offender and the ministry team, and between the ministry team and the congregation.

DEALING WITH RACIAL ISSUES AND OTHER CULTURES

In the Black community there is much bitterness about past and present racial injustices and much distrust toward people of other races, particularly White Americans. This bitterness and distrust has caused many Black ex-offenders to believe that it is a racist system that indirectly or directly resulted in their imprisonment. This belief seems to be supported by 1995 statistics from the Department of Justice. While there are more White people incarcerated in Federal and State prisons than Black people, the fact remains that under 1 percent of White people in America are imprisoned, compared with 7.38% of Black people. This has caused Black people to believe that the criminal justice system has unfairly targeted Black people.

Many prison ministries have pandered to these beliefs by stressing that a racist criminal justice system is the cause of many incarcerations rather than illegal or immoral behavior. While it may be true that the criminal justice unfairly targets blacks, there are two ways to solve the problem—either to reform the criminal justice system, or to "reform" the hearts and minds of those that it targets. You cannot catch a mouse if he goes nowhere near the trap.

Our bitterness and sensitivity to racism has caused Black people to be more tolerant and even accepting of illegal or immoral behavior among Blacks. For instance, the Black community in Washington, D.C. was up-in-arms when Marion Barry, former Mayor of Washington, D.C., was arrested for smoking crack in a downtown Washington hotel room. Suddenly, the illegal act that Barry was committing was not the issue. The issue was that the "White system" has entrapped him. When Mike Tyson was arrested after a young beauty pageant contestant accused him of raping her in a hotel room, and later when he was jailed for attacking motorists on a Maryland highway, the Black community again accused the White system of unfairly targeting Blacks. However, had Marion Barry been doing the right thing, the "entrapment" would have been fruitless, because there would have been no illegal behavior to "entrap." Had Mike Tyson been nowhere near a hotel room with the young woman, he would not have been in the position to be accused of anything. I Peter 2:13-17 clearly illustrates the benefits of practicing righteousness and obeying the law:

13Submit yourselves for the Lord's sake to every authority instituted among men: whether to the king, as the supreme authority, 14or to governors, who are sent by him to punish those who do wrong and to commend those who do right. 15For it is God's will that by doing good you should silence the ignorant talk of foolish men. 16Live as free men, but do not use your freedom as a cover-up for evil; live as servants of God. 17Show proper respect to everyone: Love the brotherhood of believers, fear God, honor the king. (NIV)

However, this fact will be lost on some Black ex-offenders you will meet. The only way to deal with it is to continue to teach about repentance through Christ and stress that it is only through the righteousness of God that racism can be dealt with. The Bible offers answers not only to those with racist beliefs, but also to those who must respond to overt or subtle racist actions or attitudes. Also, let your behavior, attitudes and actions reflect the love and acceptance of God. Whatever your race or culture, demonstrate the attitude of God by modeling acceptance of all races and cultures. Admit that there is racism in America, but demonstrate racial acceptance through embracing those who are of a different race than you and accepting and acknowledging cultural disparities.

You may have inmates or ex-offenders in your ministry who are of a different culture than yours. These cultural differences may be racial, jurisdictional, religious, or international. Your goal is to preach Christ and continue to help them grow up in the Lord, not to change their culture, despite how much their cultural practices may differ from yours. Ministering in cross-cultural situations requires acceptance, and you should not be eager to change their culture to make yours or what you think it should be. Continue to minister the Gospel, and allow the Holy Spirit to convict the ex-offender's heart about anything in their culture that may stand in the way of their relationship with God. The only time you should interfere with cultural observances and practices is if those practices are illegal or place you, your church, your ministry, or anyone else in danger.

(Scripture References: James 2:1-9, Romans 2:1-16, John 17:23, Galatians 3:28, Acts 17:26, Acts 10:34, 1 Corinthians 12:13. Also read together John 4:4, 9, 40 and Luke 10:30-37 regarding the relationship between Jews and Samaritans, and how Jesus, and even a Good Samaritan, ignored racial prejudices).

FINANCING THE EX-OFFENDER MINISTRY

Ultimately this will be the section of this manual that will most interest many people. The question is, where do we get money from and how do we keep this ministry alive financially? Unless your church has a budget that has enough money to finance an ex-offender ministry, this question is very relevant and can affect your ability to implement many of the procedures listed in this manual. I have listed several steps that should be followed if you want your ministry to be in the best position to succeed financially.

> **Maintain your relationship to the Lord through faith**
> **Start out with what you have been given**
> **Research potential financial prospects**

> **Maintain relationships and cultivate these prospects**
> **Manage the money well**
> **Stick with it**

Notice that two of the steps I mentioned above involve relationships. That is a broad stroke definition what ministry is. Ministry is building relationships with God's redeemed people, with a goal of enriching their lives in Christ. If you do not like to build relationships with people, then you should pray for that area of your life and ask the Lord for help in removing whatever is there that hinders relationship-building. If you shudder at the thought of sitting down to dinner with a man who has killed someone, this will dilute the strength of your ministry. And if you shudder at the thought of building a daily prayer life with the Lord, then you should forget this ministry altogether and seek Godly counsel for this area of your life

Maintain your relationship with the Lord through faith

Undoubtedly this is the biggest piece of financial advice I could give to anyone. In a world where financial analysts, Christian and non-Christian, are preaching the virtues of the stock market and high-paying employment and loftier degrees, my advice is simple: maintain your relationship with the Lord, and serve Him in accordance with His will. Luke 12:27-32 says:

> *27"Consider how the lilies grow. They do not labor or spin. Yet I tell you, not even Solomon in all his splendor was dressed like one of these. 28If that is how God clothes the grass of the field, which is here today, and tomorrow is thrown into the fire, how much more will he clothe you, O you of little faith! 29And do not set your heart on what you will eat or drink; do not worry about it. 30For the pagan world runs after all such things, and your Father knows that you need them. 31But seek his kingdom, and these things will be given to you as well. 32"Do not be afraid, little flock, for your Father has been pleased to give you the kingdom. (NIV)*

Seek His kingdom! Everyone involved in your ministry should be praying consistently, fasting, studying the Word, and preaching the Word, so that they will be in tune to the leading of the Holy Spirit and can keep the channels of communication open between them and the Lord. As I mentioned earlier in this manual, the word of wisdom and the word of knowledge, both gifts of the Holy Spirit, are essential in the ministry to ex-offenders. Ensure, through faith and action, that you are receiving a word from the Lord. Deuteronomy 8:18 declares that, "it is He who gives you power to make wealth." Never cut yourself off from the source of your power. Maintain your relationship.

Start out with what you have been given

You have to start with what you have been given, and trust the Lord to provide the rest. Remember, if this is truly a call on your life, the Lord will give you the tools to perform it by your faithfulness to Him. Begin with what you have, and work your way up. Some of the most powerful prison ministries in this country started with one person and a Bible, walking from cellblock to cellblock sharing the good news about Jesus to inmates. Some ex-offender ministries have started out with a basic Bible study in the basement of the church, with only two or three people present. The point is to assess what you currently have, to determine what you can do with what you have, and then to set further goals and to pray to the Lord for the financial means to meet those goals.

Research potential financial prospects
As an ex-offender ministry, you should be aware of all avenues of funding that are available to you and your ministry. I will not mention any of them here, because the list will likely be dated when you receive this manual, and the funding priorities of foundations are always changing.

If you are interested in foundation and corporate grants, you will want to start your research with the Foundation Center. The Foundation Center is a national service organization devoted to providing a single authoritative source of information on foundations and corporate giving. To reach the Foundation Center collection nearest to your area, call 1-800-424-9836. While you will be tempted to go into a Foundation Center library and ask for all the information they have on funding sources for ex-offender ministries, you will probably not find much under that category. You may want to search under alternative categories such as crime, criminal justice, mentoring, Christian programs, homelessness, etc. If your ministry focuses on meeting a particular need of ex-offenders, such as shelter, you may want to look under categories such as homelessness, economic development, etc.

Another good medium for grant research is the Internet. If you have access to the Web, you can use a search engine such as Yahoo to run searches for organizations that give grants to ministries working in criminal justice.

Be advised, however, that most non-profit organizations receive roughly less than 20% of their total giving from foundations and corporations. This is especially true of religious organizations, where most of the giving has been from individuals and estates, and very little from foundations and corporations. Some foundations, in fact, state in their giving guidelines that they do not give or religious or "sectarian" organizations. This makes the grant competition among religious organizations fiercer.

I am not writing this to discourage you from applying for foundation dollars. By all means, aggressively pursue whatever opportunities of financial support you may have. But don't bet the farm on foundations and corporations. As I mentioned, some of them will not fund religious organizations, others are leery about giving to new organizations and organizations with no track record, and others do not place outreaches to inmates and ex-offenders high on their priority list. You would do well to strategically plan your fund-raising to tap a wide range of sources, from foundations and corporations, to special events, to yard sales and car washes, to individuals and churches. In the beginning years of your ministry, work on recruiting individual donors and partnerships with churches, as well as planning special events such as concerts, plays, banquets, etc. In fact, winning a significant amount of support from other sources will make your ministry more attractive to foundations and corporations, since few of them will want to fund you if your success or failure as an organization depends entirely on their money.

Churches are an excellent source of grants and volunteers. Develop a packet of information about your ministry, then get the names and telephone numbers of every church in your area. Call the pastor on the telephone and ask him if you can send him a packet of information that describes your ministry. Be prepared to describe your calling over the phone and to tell exactly what you would like him or his church to do for you. If he requests the information, send it promptly, give him time to read it, then follow-up with another phone call.

Pursue this research with faith, knowing that it is not the research that will bless the ministry, but it is the Lord. By researching these prospects, you are not "helping out the Lord", but you are demonstrating your faith by establishing contacts with every source of income, believing the Lord will bless through one of those contacts. It may be that the Lord chooses to bless you through a person or organization you have not made previous contact with, which could be the result of your faithfulness in establishing other contacts. So be it. But never sit idly by and wait for the Lord to send people knocking on your door.

How would you advise an ex-offender who needs a job? Would you tell him to sit at home and watch TV and wait for the Lord to send an employer to ring his phone? Or would you tell him to get up, scour the newspapers, call employers, send resumes, ask friends if they have openings on their jobs, etc.? If you are intelligent, you'd advise him the latter. Similarly, how often have you gone to church expecting to hear a word from the Lord for your own life? Surely the Lord is capable of giving that word to you right then and there, but you have to get up, get dressed, get in the car and drive to church to hear the word God has planned for you. Why? Because it is the order of things in the kingdom of God that faith manifest itself with action. James 2:14-26 declares that faith without works is dead. By looking for potential funding sources, you should believe that God will bless you by your efforts.

I know that I am speaking to some of you who believe that if it is not given supernaturally, it is not a blessing from God. But God is so vast and powerful that He is able to bless us through supernatural and natural efforts, and many times, he has chosen to do so. Many of you reading this have been financially blessed of God through your employment. Some of you operate your own businesses. Through the toil of your own hands, God has blessed you financially.

Even the Bible itself is a classic hybrid of supernatural and natural effort. The word of God being revealed to man through the *supernatural* inspiration of the Holy Spirit would not have been enough to meet the Bible's purpose. These men had to take pen and paper and, through the *natural* medium of writing, record the words of God that have revealed the heart of God to every generation.

Maintain relationships and cultivate these prospects

Once you have developed these prospects, place them on your mailing list and keep them apprised of the developments of your ministry. Tell them about your needs and **invite** them to participate through prayer, volunteer work or direct financial giving. Never try to make anyone give. Giving should always be done by invitation, never by demand. It is interesting that tithes and offerings are never commanded in the Bible. They are an invitation to participate in the financial blessings of God through sacrificial giving. All you can do is to preach the word through the efforts of your ministry. If people are blessed, they will give.

It has been said that fund-raising should be renamed friend-raising. The primary focus of ministry is not to raise money or to meet the budget, but to build relationships. Through the relationships you have developed, the money will come, as long as you remain true to the Word. There are few people who will open their checkbook and write out a $1000 check to an organization or person that they barely know. Most giving is based on relationship. Your responsibility here is to make sure that your contacts are kept up-to-date on the ministry. Never let them wonder what is going on. If you ministry has news to share, or events to promote, your contacts should know about it before anyone else does. Make them a part of your organization.

Every person you contact through the ministry should be placed on your mailing list and responded to promptly. Return every phone call, and answer every letter (if you have developed a ministry team as I mentioned above, you could appoint one or more people for these tasks). Treat every person that comes into contact with your ministry as the most important person on your agenda that day. Remember that your ministry is about building relationships.

It is also off-putting to try to develop a relationship with someone who clearly wants nothing to do with you. If any of your prospects ask you not to contact them anymore, for whatever reason, remove them from your mailing list and place them on your prayer list. If anyone on your mailing list has not requested to be placed on it, send them a letter describing your ministry and ask if they can remain on your mailing list. If they respond no, remove them immediately. You do not want to annoy people, and unsolicited mail can get annoying (not to mention that it probably will not get read, which will be a waste of your paper and postage). If they do not respond at all, send a follow-up letter. If they respond no, or do not respond at all to the follow-up, remove them from the list. If they are interested in your ministry, they will have no problem receiving your mail.

Manage the money well

Once you receive money, it is essential that you manage it in accordance with Biblical principles. Many ministries have failed not because they did not have enough money, but because they failed to use it and manage it properly. It is important that you cast away all outdated ideals and strategies about money management.

Below, I have listed some principles of successful money management that can be applied to ministries. It doesn't matter whether the ministry is a two-person operation or a conglomerate of hundreds of people. God has a lot to say about finances in the Bible, and it is important that we know what the word of God says about this vital subject.

There was poverty in Israel because the people failed to act according to their faith. They failed to believe that God would take care of them and bless them, even though He had done so many times before. Even today, poverty and financial struggle exists because people fail to act according to the will of God. Below are proven Biblical principles of stewardship that, when followed, will put your ministry on the road to financial freedom and help you to eliminate or prevent many financial problems. Many of the principles apply directly to the personal finances of the person or people in charge of the ministry, as well as the finances of the ministry itself

- a) Make sure that anyone in charge of receiving or distributing money is a person of character and integrity.
- b) Begin to give according to your ability. Tithes and offerings acknowledge God's providence and trust (Proverbs 3:9-10, Malachi 3:8-12).
- c) Give yourselves to God first, then give liberally, not forgetting about the poor (*2 Corinthians 8:1-24, 9:1-15*).
- d) Pay all taxes on time. Do not avoid taxes, or cheat on them (*Matthew 22:15-21, Romans 13:1-7, I Peter 2:13-17*).
- e) Establish savings (Luke 16:19-31, Proverbs 21:20)
- f) Establish a system of planned spending, including budgeting, debt reduction, and being aware of the ministry's financial condition (*Proverbs 27:23-24, James 4:13-14, Proverbs 22:7, Romans 13:8*).
- g) Avoid greed and lavish spending (*Eccl. 5:10, Luke 12:15, James 4:1-3*).
- h) Pay all bills on time (*Romans 13:8*).

This sounds like dumb advice. Obviously, if people could pay their bills on time, they would. The problem is, many can't, because of mismanagement of money. Proper financial planning eliminates this problem.

- i) Stop all nonessential spending.

Stick with it

Even with the advice I have given below, you may find your ministry to be lacking in dollars and prospects. Even as I write this, our ministry continues to battle to bring in finances. But a simple statement becomes the focus of our work. *Persevere in the time of storm.*

Once one September, I look at the finances and discovered that we were getting low in cash. Money trickled in, a few checks here and there, but nothing that could keep pace with the expenses of our ministry. As a testimony to our financial management skills, we operated for two years on a couple of grants we had received in 1996, a year after we officially started our ministry. But that money was quickly running out, and we had no prospects for any more money. We were faced with having to shut down our office because we could not afford to pay the rent. And I knew that if God did not move on our behalf, the ministry doors would be closing its doors by the end of the year.

As I pondered this situation, I called a Board meeting, with the intent to explain our financial position. Before we got into Board business, I announced that we would stop the meeting in time to allow us to pray for fifteen minutes for the finances of the ministry. And we did just that. We prayed fervently for our finances, for the proposals we had sent out to area foundations, and those we were going to send out. We prayed for ourselves, that God would keep us encouraged during this trial.

Three months later, as our money tanks ran empty and we literally functioned on financial *fumes*, a call came in from a foundation director. She said that her Board of Trustees had voted, and were pleased to approve us a grant for $5000! Not only that, her Board mentioned that our organization had presented to them one of the best proposals they had seen in many years! God truly moved on our behalf, but that was not all. Three weeks later, another foundation sent us a check for an additional $5000! We believe it was because we prayed, remained steadfast, and allowed the Lord to move on our behalf. Sometimes the Lord will allow us to get into situations where we have no other choice but to depend on Him. Even when things look bleak, God is faithful to deliver.

PEDOPHILES AND SEX OFFENDERS

Among the class of ex-offenders, no other group evokes more negative public reaction than pedophiles, child abusers, and sex offenders. So strong is the reaction to this group of offenders, particularly pedophiles, that many people would rather have a murderer living in their community that a pedophile. This public outcry has resulted in the passage of several laws that affected the post-release status and activities of those convicted of crimes against children. Your ministry needs to be aware of these laws and how they will impact any pedophile or sex offender to whom you minister.

Megan's Law:
This law[5] amended a portion of the Violent Crime Control and Law Enforcement Act of 1994[6] to allow information collected under state sex offender registration programs to be released to the public. Law enforcement officials are required to notify neighbors when a convicted sex offender moves into their neighborhood, and a convicted sex offender can be rearrested if he refuses to register with the sex offender registry where he lives. This law was named after Megan Kanka, a 7-year-old New Jersey girl who was raped and murdered in 1994 by a convicted sex offender living in her neighborhood. Most states in the U.S. have modified their sex-offender registry laws because of this Act.

Kansas Sexual Predator Law
A case before the Supreme Court in 1997 involved a Kansas law that gave the courts authority to confine sex offenders to mental institutions, even if the sex offenders had

served all of their prison time. The law specifically provided that a sex offender, if he was "mentally abnormal" (defined as the likelihood the offender will continue to commit crimes against children), could be committed to a mental institution.

The opposition to this law came from a convicted sex offender, Leroy Hendricks, who had a 30-year record of molesting children. His defense, which was upheld by the Kansas Supreme Court, was that the law amounted to "double jeopardy," the legal term for being punished twice for the same crime.

The Supreme Court disagreed, however, saying that it was not "double punishment" for a convicted sex offender to have completed his sentence, and then confined to a mental institution if there was a likelihood he would continue to molest children. The majority upheld the Kansas law, paving the way for other states to place similar sexual predator laws on their books.

As a minister I agree with both of these laws. Anyone who has harmed children or has the potential to harm children should be watched very closely. As an ex-offender minister dealing with child abusers, you have a double-duty. You have a duty to reach out to the offender, offering God's love and getting him into the word of God and around supportive, understanding people on a daily basis. But you also have a duty to protect the children. Child sex offenders prey on children because they are weak, innocent and powerless. Adult sex victims, to an extent, have the potential to defend themselves. Children do not. Therefore, you must be the defender of these children, with the parents, to protect them against any possible relapse. You should make it a policy of your ministry that anyone convicted of a sex crime should show proof of registry with the authorities before joining your ministry.

There is no one that God cannot heal, including sex offenders. However, because of the sensitivity of this issue and the natural inclination of parents to protect their children from anything that could be potentially dangerous, you need to be more responsible than just bringing a sex offender into your church or ministry and saying "I know God has healed them." Sex offenders often have deep-rooted demonic spirits that have entered them during childhood, probably after having been sexually abused themselves. A prayer of deliverance may be successful in removing the demonic spirits that have afflicted the life of a sex offender. But once that spirit is gone, there is a cleanup process involved that can take a very long time, and maybe the rest of his life.

The parable of the man repossessed shows what often happens when a sex offender is delivered from demonic influence:

> *Now when the unclean spirit goes out of a man, it passes through waterless places, seeking rest, and does not find it. Then it says, "I will return to my house from which I came"; and when it comes, it finds it unoccupied, swept, and put in order. Then it goes and takes along with it seven other spirits more wicked than itself, and they go in and live there; and the last state of*

that man becomes worse than the first. That is the way it will also be with this evil generation. (Matthew 12:43-45, NAS).

It is very common for a sex offender to be delivered from demonic influence, only to have the demonic spirits return. Why? Because the house was unoccupied. Nothing or no one was living there. Naturally, the demons felt they had a right to return. They *do not* have a right to return, but because it is the nature of demons to kill, steal and to destroy, they will always squat on unoccupied real estate that is not legally theirs.

It is important for the sex offender to keep his house occupied and clean with the word and the spirit of the Lord, and to remove from him any distractions that could cause him to relapse. Only a trained Christian counselor who knows the word of God and who is spiritually discerning and mature should deal with sex offenders and keep them accountable. The sex offender should always be surrounded with fellowship and support, while removing him from any potentially dangerous situations. For instance, if he is a pedophile, under no circumstances should he be allowed in a situation where he is unsupervised with or has control over children.

The ex-offender may feel that because of the restrictions placed on him, that you do not trust him. However, it is not an issue of trust; it's an issue of treatment. A pedophile is obviously weak in the area of his sexual attraction to children. Any area that is weak in an ex-offender's life (or in anyone's life, for that matter), needs to be isolated until full healing and strength has taken place. For instance, a drug addict should not be allowed to smell, taste or see drugs. An alcohol should never be in a situation where he has easy access to booze. An embezzler should probably not work in a bank or other area where he has to deal with money. These areas should be isolated, quarantined, and bandaged with the word of God and with the Holy Spirit, until the area has been completely healed and the ex-offender demonstrates the fruits of the Spirit in his or her life.

CHAPTER FOUR

Love, Discipleship, and Ministry

GODLY LOVE TOWARD THE EX-OFFENDER-WHAT DOES IT MEAN?

As a minister who is young enough to vividly remember my times growing up with my mother, I believe that the love of a parent for her child is the best example of the love that should be shown to an ex-offender. It also parallels the love that God has for us. The Bible talks about God's parental relationship with us by declaring that "The Spirit himself testifies with our spirit that we are God's children (Romans 8:16)" (NIV). Those who are led by the Spirit are "the sons of God" (Romans 8:14). Therefore, God is our Father, we are His children, and He loves and provides for us.

Parental love is not perfect, nor can it equal the love God has for His children. But it can reveal some truths about the perfect love God has for His children and the love that we should show to ex-offenders. Many charities and ministries have equated the word "love" with "giving." This is true in a sense. After all, the love that a mother or father has for a child requires "giving" the child everything the child needs for growth and development. But on the other hand, parental love requires *denying* the child anything that can hurt or hinder the child's growth. Therefore, love is as much *denying* as it is *giving*.

Many charities have forgotten this. They believe that love involves giving selflessly, without realizing that their giving, even if meant well, could hinder growth rather than help it. If the person cannot handle what is given, or intends to use the gift in as destructive rather than a productive manner, then the gift becomes the tool that aids the destruction. How many of us have given loose change to a beggar on the street, believing that he was going to use the money for food? But instead, the man went into a liquor store and bought a bottle of Wild Irish Rose. The money that was handed out unchecked, in the name of love, has actually helped to foster the man's alcoholism. It might have been better to deny the money, but to buy the man some food, or better still, point the man to a shelter or soup kitchen in the area where he could receive help. This may not be what the man wants, but it is a better help to him than subsidizing the man's alcoholism.

With ex-offenders, love can be as much denying as giving. Earlier, I recommended that cash, or any cash equivalent, not be given to any ex-offender, no matter how much he insists on it. Why? Because to give cash gives the ex-offender freedom and temptation to buy whatever he wants. Even though he may say it is to pay rent, or to buy groceries, or to catch a cab to work, cash affords an ex-offender many options, some of which he may not be able to handle.

I cite a case where an ex-offender was given $250 cash by a ministry to pay the rent. The person who gave him the money trusted him enough to hand him the cash without getting a signed receipt. When he left the ministry's office, he had every intention of paying the rent. But as he caught the bus on the way to the rental office, he saw an old girlfriend board the bus. She recognized him, sat down beside him, and they began to talk about old times. Suddenly, the ex-offender lost interest in going to the rental office, but went to his old girlfriend's neighborhood to talk with some of his old buddies and catch up with their lives. Encouraged by the possibility of a renewed romantic relationship with his old girlfriend, he hung out with his buddies and his old girlfriend for the rest of the evening. They went out, partied, drank and did drugs, all paid for with the $250.00 in the ex-offender's pocket.

He was eventually evicted from his apartment. He moved in with his girlfriend, but left after they had an argument. He went back to his buddies, did more drugs, and eventually got arrested for trying to rob a convenience store.

What role did the $250 pay in all of this? Maybe he would have still been arrested if the $250 were not given to him. Maybe things would have turned out the same. But the $250 was valuable money taken out of the hands of the people of God and given to drug dealers. Money that could have been used to feed and clothe someone was used to finance a thriving drug trade.

It is important to remember that many ex-offenders coming out of prison are infants in the Lord. They have to start over. Everything that is given to them should be fittingly rationed to ensure that no harm is caused. This includes the word of God. The Scripture says, "Do not give dogs what is sacred; do not throw your pearls to pigs. If you do, they may trample them under their feet, and then turn and tear you to pieces" (Matthew 7:6, NIV). They may say, "I can handle this, or I can handle that." Don't automatically believe it. Unless they have been tested and proven in finances (a good test is the ability to get and keep a job and to budget effectively), avoid giving cash or cash equivalents for any reason.

Another issue that is just a controversial as money is the issue of time. One thing that is sure to wreck havoc with many of your ex-offenders is having too much time on their hands. The Scripture warns against being idle (Proverbs 21:25-26, 2 Thessalonians 3:8-11, Proverbs 14:23). Therefore, your ex-offenders should spend most of their time working, looking for work, training for work, or doing something that keeps them busy and involved. There should be activities planned during non-working hours as well. Try to keep your ex-offenders involved in the church and involved in fellowship. Give them a task in the church. Plan dinners. Set up a support group. Keep them active and involved. It is not the time the ex-offender spends with you that will draw them down. It is the time the ex-offender spends *away* from you. While you may not be able to be with them 24 hours a day, seven days a week, you should be aware of their whereabouts always.

Of course, an ideal situation would be to have a transitional housing center for ex-offenders. In this housing situation, you can set a curfew and arrange a structured schedule that allows the ex-offender little time for idle-mindedness. Without such an arrangement, it may be difficult to enforce curfews or schedules.

You may wonder why I insist on being so restrictive with ex-offenders. It was the lack of self-control that resulted in many persons being locked up in prison. Naturally, some training in self-control needs to be put in place with a program of discipleship.

DISCIPLESHIP FOR THE EX-OFFENDER: Leaving the Nets

The call to discipleship is given in Mark 1:17, when Jesus, while walking along the Sea of Galilee, says to the fisherman Simon and his brother Andrew, "Come, follow me, and I will make you fishers of men." The Scripture declares that Simon and his brother immediately left their nets and followed Jesus. In this Scripture, we have the basic definition and elements of discipleship, which I will discuss below as they relate to the ministry to ex-offenders:

   a. Jesus Christ initiates the call to discipleship.
   b. Discipleship is to follow Jesus and His word.
   c. Discipleship involves putting aside everything that could stand in the way of following Jesus.
   d. The goal of discipleship is to develop Christian character and to produce men and women who are equipped to disciple others.

Jesus Christ initiates the call to discipleship.
It is impossible for an ex-offender to be discipled unless he first receives Jesus Christ as His Lord and Savior. The very nature of discipleship requires an unwavering and committed relationship to the one who is to be followed in discipleship, who is Jesus.

Discipleship is to follow Jesus and His Word.
John 8:31-32 says, "*To the Jews who had believed him, Jesus said, 'If you hold to my teaching, you are really my disciples. Then you will know the truth, and the truth will set you free'*" (NIV). Discipleship involves not only hearing the word of God, but also obeying the word of God. With discipleship, obedience to the Word is the order of the day. No one can truly say he is a disciple unless he is obedient to the word of God.

In the world today, there are many people who profess to be Christian, but are not obedient to the word of God. I have seen many people who could talk as well as the best preachers, and who could quote Scriptures at the drop of a hat. However, these same people constantly and deliberately lived their lives in disobedience to the very Scriptures they quote so well.

I would not be so bold to suggest that ex-offenders who undergo discipleship training will immediately drop all of their vices. Because we are flesh, we will blow it from time to time. We will make mistakes. We will grow at different rates. However, holding to the teachings of Jesus should involve not just an intellectual exercise. True disciples of Jesus are those who hold the teachings of Jesus in their hearts. True disciples of Jesus want to know the Word and to obey the Word (Psalms 119:97). Since they are flesh, they will make mistakes. But they will not want to make mistakes. They will want to obey the word of God.

Discipleship for ex-offenders should involve training in the Word of God. Regular Bible studies should be set up for ex-offenders. These studies should be held at least once or twice a week. As a starting point, these studies can cover the elementary foundation principles of the Christian faith found in Hebrews 6:1-2. These principles are *Repentance from Dead Works, Faith toward God, the Doctrine of Baptisms, Laying on of Hands, Resurrection of the Dead,* and *Eternal Judgment.* Mentors should also meet with the ex-offender at least once a week and study the Bible with him.

At least for the first three months, your discipleship-training program should be so intensive that the ex-offender has little time for anything else other than studying and receiving the Word of God. This is not meant as a controlling tactic, but is meant to bathe the ex-offender in the Word of God. The more the ex-offender studies the word of God under the guidance of the Holy Spirit, the more the word will take root in his heart. As the Scripture says in Hebrews 4:12, *"For the word of God is living and active. Sharper than any double-edged sword, it penetrates even to dividing soul and spirit, joints and marrow; it judges the thoughts and attitudes of the heart"* (NIV).

Discipleship involves putting aside everything that could stand in the way of following Jesus.

When Simon and his brother Andrew left their nets and immediately followed Jesus, they did something that in modern times would have been consider crazy, even suicidal. Imagine leaving a good, well-paying job just to follow Jesus. Would you do it? Yet, that's just what the fisherman did. There was something so compelling about Jesus that they left their careers to sit at the feet of Jesus and to be two of the twelve men that would continue Jesus' work after his resurrection. Their faith in this man was so great that they willingly followed him without hesitation. Consider this passage from Matthew 10:32-39:

> *"Whoever acknowledges me before men, I will also acknowledge him before my Father in heaven. But whoever disowns me before men, I will disown him before my Father in heaven.*
> *"Do not suppose that I have come to bring peace to the earth. I did not come to bring peace, but a sword. For I have come to turn*
>
> *" `a man against his father,*
> *a daughter against her mother,*
> *a daughter-in-law against her mother-in-law--*
> *a man's enemies will be the members of his own household.'*
>
> *"Anyone who loves his father or mother more than me is not worthy of me; anyone who loves his son or daughter more than me is not worthy of me; and anyone who does not take his cross and follow me is not worthy of me. Whoever finds his life will lose it, and whoever loses his life for my sake will find it"* (NIV).

So, what is the lesson in all this? Does our relationship with Jesus require giving up our jobs, our careers, our families, and our friends? Perhaps. Certainly there are jobs that can draw us away from the Lord if we are not strong enough to handle them. Our families and our friends can draw us away as well. For an ex-offender, all of these things can work toward his destruction if he places them above Jesus. If his desire to make money, or his desire to reunite with an old girlfriend, is greater than his desire to know Jesus, he is well on the road to failure. The point is to love Jesus above everything else.

I have noticed, in dealing with reentrants who need employment, that often the only job they are offered is a job that involves working on the day that they should be in church. It takes a person in tune with the Lord to recognize whether a job is a true blessing or just an attempt from the devil to draw the person away from the fellowship of the saints. In general, I would recommend structuring your ex-offender ministry so the ex-offender receives at least three months of unencumbered training. Getting a job, getting back with a girlfriend or wife, or any other concerns should be placed on a shelf until the ex-offender has had time to cement his relationship with Jesus. This "honeymoon" period should be a time of consecration and study of the Scriptures to build faith and spiritual stamina. If this faith and stamina is not built, your efforts to employ him may be contradictory to your efforts to build him up in the most holy faith of Jesus Christ.

Hebrews 12:1-3 is good advice to follow:

> *Therefore, since we are surrounded by such a great cloud of witnesses, let us throw off everything that hinders and the sin that so easily entangles, and let us run with perseverance the race marked out for us. Let us fix our eyes on Jesus, the author and perfecter of our faith, who for the joy set before him endured the cross, scorning its shame, and sat down at the right hand of the throne of God. Consider him who endured such opposition from sinful men, so that you will not grow weary and lose heart (NIV).*

The goal of discipleship is to develop Christian character and to produce men and women who are equipped to disciple others.
John 15:1-8 reads as follows:

"I am the true vine, and my Father is the gardener. He cuts off every branch in me that bears no fruit, while every branch that does bear fruit he prunes so that it will be even more fruitful. You are already clean because of the word I have spoken to you. Remain in me, and I will remain in you. No branch can bear fruit by itself; it must remain in the vine. Neither can you bear fruit unless you remain in me.

"I am the vine; you are the branches. If a man remains in me and I in him, he will bear much fruit; apart from me you can do nothing. If anyone does not remain in me, he is like a branch that is thrown away and withers; such branches are picked up, thrown into the fire and burned. If you remain in me and my words remain in you, ask whatever you wish, and it will be given you. This is to my Father's glory, that you bear much fruit, showing yourselves to be my disciples" (NIV).

One of the characteristics of a true disciple is to be a fruit-bearer. To achieve this, the true disciple must "remain in the vine," which is Jesus. The term *remain* implies constancy and commitment. To bear fruit, the branch must remain, or be constantly attached, to the vine.

The process of being discipled never ends for a Christian in this life. Discipleship is endless. Discipleship training may last for a definite period of time, but *being a disciple* is a lifestyle. Everything that I mentioned above--acknowledging His call to discipleship, holding to the teaching of Jesus, and putting Jesus first in everything-- is an everyday process. As the ex-offender abides in the vine and continues to grow as a disciple, God will begin to produce the "fruits of the Spirit" within him. (Galatians 5:22-23.) Once he begins to bear the fruits, he can lead others to Christ by demonstrating the fruits in his own life. An ex-offender who bears the fruit of the Spirit is a powerful influence in ex-offender ministry. This is extremely important, since ex-offenders are often more accepting of fellow ex-offenders because of their common experiences. God is raising up an army of formerly incarcerated men and women who are equipped to go into the prisons and onto the streets and "make disciples of all the nations, baptizing them in the name of the Father and of the Son and of the Holy Spirit, and teaching them to obey everything I have commanded you." (Matthew 28:19-20, NIV).

THE PRUNING PROCESS: HOW TO DEAL WITH SUFFERING

Being a branch abiding in the vine of Jesus involves a process known as pruning. If you are a gardener, you are familiar with this term. Pruning involves cutting or trimming parts of a branch to improve its shape or its ability to bear fruit. If the branch were not bearing fruit, it would be cut off completely. The only branches that are pruned are those that bear fruit and are worth saving.

For many ex-offenders, your ex-offender ministry will be one big, long pruning process. The goal is to encourage Christian growth while cutting away everything that could hinder growth. Unfortunately, the cutting away process is often painful, and there is a natural inclination in humans to avoid this suffering at all costs.

The quality of your ex-offender ministry will be determined not only by how you handle them when times are going well, but when times of suffering come. Your ex-offenders will experience a gamut of feelings ranging from despair and discouragement to outright bitterness and anger. They will be tempted to return to their former lifestyles. They will be disheartened if they are unable to find jobs because of their criminal history. They will feel that your program is too restrictive. They will doubt the promises of the word and seek out the promises of the world. They will want to hang around their former friends. They will deal with rejection from family and friends. All of these are part of the painful pruning process that will help them bear more fruit and grow into better Christians.

Do not become over-sympathetic and try to spare ex-offenders the unavoidable pain that comes because of the pruning process. Instead, *walk with them through the pain.* Your job as a minister is not to try to take the pain away, because you can't. That's God's job. Your job is to help the ex-offender endure the pain. Through prayer, fellowship, Bible study and counseling, you can help the ex-offender realize that his pain will be temporary, producing a stronger, more mature Christian, reflecting the glory of God. As Romans 8:18 says, *"I consider that our present sufferings are not worth comparing with the glory that will be revealed in us"* (NIV). Also read 2 Corinthians 1:3-11. The minister must be prepared to patiently encourage and exhort, knowing that each trial the ex-offender goes through will likely place on him the temptation to give up, to go back to the streets.

You must keep the ex-offender focused, constantly reminding him that God is with him. Continually challenge him to pray and to seek God earnestly, and reject any attempts to brush off times of fellowship, Bible study, corporate worship and prayer. One of the enemy's most used tactics is to try to woo the ex-offender away from his source of strength, encouragement and love. Many times, the demonic strategy will be to replace times of gathering with legitimate things like jobs, school, spending time with the kids, etc. If this is left unchecked, the ex-offender will spend less and less time around the saints, leaving him open and vulnerable to the devil's attack. This is a reason I recommend that for the first three months (longer, if possible) of an ex-offender's involvement with your ministry, he is allowed to do little else but focus on the word of God. Seemingly legitimate and necessary things could cause too great of a distraction during this period, and could even draw the immature ex-offender away from his studies and away from the faith.

I must stress again that the ex-offender's relationship with Jesus is the most important thing to work on at this point. It is urgent that the inner man be changed. It is the natures of many charitable groups to give money, jobs, food, shelter, and clothes to ex-offenders and believe that they are making a difference. But more important than these things should be helping the ex-offender grow in the knowledge of Christ and helping him deal with any sin problem that afflicts him.

I spoke about the importance of Bible study in the section on discipleship, above. Ex-offenders need to be bathed in the word of God, for it is through the word that their faith will increase. All counseling needs to be based on the word of God.

> **2 Timothy 3:10-17** *You, however, know all about my teaching, my way of life, my purpose, faith, patience, love, endurance, 11persecutions, sufferings--what kinds of things happened to me in Antioch, Iconium and Lystra, the persecutions I endured. Yet the Lord rescued me from all of them. 12In fact, everyone who wants to live a godly life in Christ Jesus will be persecuted, 13while evil men and impostors will go from bad to worse, deceiving and being deceived. 14But as for you, continue in what you have learned and have become convinced of, because you know those from whom you learned it, 15and how from infancy you have known the holy Scriptures, which are able to make you wise for salvation through faith in Christ Jesus. 16All Scripture is God-breathed and is useful for teaching, rebuking, correcting and training in righteousness, 17so that the man of God may be thoroughly equipped for every good work (NIV).*

THE SCRIPTURAL BASIS FOR THE MINISTRY TO INMATES AND EX-OFFENDERS

"Do not gloat when your enemy falls; when he stumbles, do not let your heart rejoice." Proverbs 24:17 (NIV).

Many people are reluctant to place inmates and ex-offenders in the category of "disadvantaged" that has been traditionally reserved for the poor, the elderly, at-risk children, people on welfare, and even the victims of these same inmates and ex-offenders. They will say that these men and women deserve whatever punishment they are given and do not deserve our compassion. They will even show you Scriptures to suggest that God, especially in the Old Testament, dealt firmly with criminals. Some will say that the death penalty of today is validated by Biblical examples of stoning, beheading, and crucifixion. So the question is, should the church have compassion on criminals? If so, what is the Scriptural mandate for this?

Obviously you know my answer to the first question is yes; otherwise there would have been no reason to write this manual. The church *should* and *must* have compassion on criminals, if for no other reason than God had compassion on us by sending Jesus Christ to the cross to die on our stead. Should we dare treat God's compassion for us so lightly by suggesting that criminals are not deserving of that same compassion?

Now, you may be offended by that comparison. Maybe the worst thing you've ever done was stealing a gumdrop from a candy store, or jaywalking on a city street. But murder, rape, abortion, or stealing candy from a store is an act committed because of SIN. The only way to deal with sin is to confront it with the word of God. Jesus Christ dealt with our sin by paying the ultimate penalty of death, so through His redemptive blood, we could be reunited with God. Thus, as recipients of the grace and mercy of God, we are called to "go ye into all the world, and preach the gospel to every creature." (Mark 16:15, KJV). The classic Scripture is Matthew 25:35-40, which classifies "prisoners" as the "least of these my brethren" and states that through visiting prisoners, you are in effect visiting Jesus. The hungry, the thirsty, the naked, the stranger, the sick, and the prisoner—all are considered so important to Jesus that He says serving them and caring for their needs is the same as *serving Him*.

Another classic example is found in the Epistle of Paul to Philemon. Here, Paul meets Onesimus, a runaway slave of Philemon, while he and Onesimus were in prison. Paul makes an appeal to Philemon on behalf of Onesimus, asking the slave owner to forgive Onesimus of any trespasses and to accept him back not just as a slave, but as a brother in the Lord. This short epistle illustrates the mandate of the church in responding to those who have wronged us. The mandate is forgiveness. The church should stand ready to forgive and accept anyone who has wronged us, no matter what the offense may be. However, to do this requires a tremendous faith in the Lord and a dependence on the Holy Spirit, because some offenses are too atrocious to forgive on our own accord. But it must be done, not only for the sake of the many inmates and ex-offenders who need to be accepted, but also for your own sake. Luke 6:27-37 reads as follows:

> *27"But I tell you who hear me: Love your enemies, do good to those who hate you, 28bless those who curse you, pray for those who mistreat you. 29If someone strikes you on one cheek, turn to him the other also. If someone takes your cloak, do not stop him from taking your tunic. 30Give to everyone who asks you, and if anyone takes what belongs to you, do not demand it back. 31Do to others as you would have them do to you. 32"If you love those who love you, what credit is that to you? Even `sinners' love those who love them. 33And if you do good to those who are good to you, what credit is that to you? Even `sinners' do that. 34And if you lend to those from whom you expect repayment, what credit is that to you? Even `sinners' lend to `sinners,' expecting to be repaid in full. 35But love your enemies, do good to them, and lend to them without expecting to get anything back. Then your reward will be great, and you will be sons of the Most High, because he is kind to the ungrateful and wicked. 36Be merciful, just as your Father is merciful. 37"Do not judge, and you will not be judged. Do not condemn, and you will not be condemned. Forgive, and you will be forgiven (NIV).*

As you can see, forgiveness is a command, not an option. Failure to forgive and extend the love of God to those who have committed crimes affects not only the perpetrator, but the wronged as well. Whether the crime was committed against us personally, against others, or against the church or society at large, the church, through the Holy Spirit, must reach out to inmates and ex-offenders. If we do not, it will block our own blessings from God. Consider verse 37 above and also Matthew 6:12-14. If we desire to reap God's blessings on ourselves, on our families and on our ministries, we cannot afford to write people off because they have committed a crime.

Many opinions about criminal justice today, especially among Christians, are shaped by the laws in Leviticus, which called for "an eye for an eye" and prescribed the death penalty for murder, rape, abortion, kidnapping and certain religious crimes such as sorcery or dishonoring the Sabbath. Some people believe that a return to the "strict" criminal justice system that existed in Israel is warranted today in response to the astronomical crime rates. But this thinking is based on fear. People naturally want the government to do anything they can to reduce or eliminate crime, because they are afraid to come out at night. They are afraid to open their doors to strangers. They walk their children to school everyday because of the fear of abduction.

YES, we need to protect ourselves from criminals. But we also need to recognize that the crime problem in America today is not because the government has failed to build more jails or to enact the death penalty. Crime is the result of SIN in the human heart. Therefore, the most effective and promising response to the problem of crime in America is to change hearts. This is why Jesus, in Matthew 5:38-41 says that we are not to resist an evil person. Vengeance, in any form, is not allowed for the Christian. Whether that vengeance be exacted through the physical taking of life, or through treating the inmate or ex-offender harshly, or through a lack of forgiveness, we are commanded to avoid it. Even in early Israel, the strict system of punishments for crimes was exacted because God loves His people and wants for us to live in harmony with Him and with one another. But these penalties were not acts of vengeance—they were simply penalties. Forgiveness of sins was always available even to one whom was given the death penalty. Remember the criminal who hung next to Jesus on Calvary. Jesus forgave him and said to him, "Today, you shall be with me in paradise." (Luke 23:43).

The mission of the church is restoring souls. Clearly the benefits of this are greater than locking criminals up for life or executing them in a gas chamber. Rev. Kenneth Copeland has written the following statement:

> *Satan is not worried about God. He is postponing that inevitable confrontation as long as he can. But since we represent God's divine power and authority in the world, the adversary must reckon with **us**. If a person were to die now, the devil would not care whether he went to heaven or hell. Either way, he would be forever removed from the field of battle and out of his way. What Satan **does** fear is a person who is alive, one who has God's divine nature in his spirit. Only such*

a person can wield the sword of the Spirit--the Word of God—with accuracy. We are dangerous to him, and we will have to resist him.[7]

How true! Is it any wonder that discussions about the death penalty have resurfaced in recent years. Satan's desire is to frustrate the efforts of God by removing inmates and ex-offenders from the battlefield, from any possibility of joining the Lord's camp. He knows that an inmate or an ex-offender, once turned over to the Lord, can be a very dangerous weapon in the arsenal of God. A former criminal, armed with the word of God, is in an excellent position to win many more former criminals to Christ, simply because he knows the territory. He knows how criminals think. He knows the streets. He understands their emotions, thoughts, and attitudes. And inmates and ex-offenders will listen to him, because he understands them. He knows what attitudes they respond to, what inflections of voice that will cause them to listen. Satan does not want a man like this in God's army at any cost!

This is why it is so difficult for ex-offenders when they are released. Satan desires to keep them so bound that they will never enter the kingdom of God. Satan puts disdain and fear in the hearts of employers so they will not hire ex-offenders. He puts disgust and fear into the hearts of homeowners so they will not allow an ex-offender to move into their neighborhood (particularly if they are sex offenders or child abusers). He has caused the hearts of God's people to place more value on property than people, to the point that many churches will not allow an ex-offender into their congregation for fear he might steal something. Even if the ex-offender accepts Jesus while in prison and continues to fellowship with the Lord after release, Satan's' plan is to frustrate them so much that they will backslide right into the enemy's territory. But if the ex-offender survives the onslaught of Satan, he will be a dangerous opponent to Satan. Therefore, the church cannot afford to ignore the mission field of criminal justice. Every single person released from prison, not matter what the crime, has the potential to strike a mighty blow directly in the eye of Satan. The people of God need to ensure that they reach this potential, rather than voting out of fear to lock them up and execute them.

SCRIPTURES RELATED TO PRISONERS:

Genesis 39:11-41:14:	Joseph falsely accused of attempted rape and his experience in prison.
Genesis 42:15-20:	Joseph imprisons his brothers.
Genesis 45:4-8:	Joseph reveals himself to his brothers.
Numbers 21:1:	King of Arad imprisons some of the Israelites.
Judges 16:21-25:	Samson blinded and imprisoned.
1 Kings 22:27:	Micaiah imprisoned because of his prophecy.
2 Kings 17:4:	Hoshea, king of Israel imprisoned by the king of

	Assyria for being a traitor.
2 Kings 24:10-12:	Jehoiachin, king of Israel, taken prisoner by Nebuchadnezzar.
2 Kings 25:27-30:	Jehoiachin released from prison by Evil-Merodach, new king of Babylon.
2 Chronicles 16:7-10:	Hanani the seer imprisoned by Asa King of Judah for giving a bad prophesy.
2 Chronicles 18:26:	Micaiah imprisoned by Ahab, king of Israel, because of his prophecy.
Psalm 69:33:	The Lord does not despise prisoners.
Psalm 79:11 and 102:20:	A request for the Lord to preserve those condemned to die.
Psalm 146:7:	The Lord sets prisoners free.
Isaiah 14:17:	Satan does not allow his captives to go home.
Isaiah 24:21-22:	The kings of the earth are imprisoned.
Isaiah 42:7:	The foretelling of Jesus' coming to set free the captives in prison.
Isaiah 49:9:	In the day of salvation the Lord will tell captives to come and those in darkness to be free.
Isaiah 53:8:	Jesus' imprisonment foretold.
Isaiah 61:1:	The proclamation of the Lord's anointed to announce freedom for prisoners.
Jeremiah 32:1-2:	Jeremiah imprisoned in Judah.
Jeremiah 32:6-15:	Jeremiah buys a field while in prison.
Jeremiah 33:	The Lord speaks to Jeremiah while he is in prison.
Jeremiah 36:5:	Jeremiah dictated the Lord's Word to Baruch during his imprisonment.
Jeremiah 36:26:	Jehoiakim tries to have Jeremiah arrested.
Jeremiah 37:4-38:13:	Falsely accused of desertion, Jeremiah is beaten and imprisoned.
Jeremiah 38:28:	Jeremiah continues his imprisonment until Jerusalem is captured.
Jeremiah 40:1-4:	Jeremiah is freed by the imperial guard.
Jeremiah 52:11:	Zedekiah king of Jerusalem, blinded and imprisoned for life by the king of Babylon.
Jeremiah 52:31-34:	Jehoiachin, King of Judah, released from prison by the king of Babylon.

Lamentations 3:34:	God does not willingly crush prisoners.
Lamentations 3:53-55:	Jeremiah pleads with God during his imprisonment.
Daniel 3:1-28:	Shadrach, Meshach, and Abednego imprisoned, thrown into the furnace and rescued by God
Daniel 6:16-24:	Daniel thrown into the lion's den and rescued by the Lord.
Zechariah 9:11-12:	God's promise to deliver prisoners.
Matthew 4:12:	John the Baptist imprisoned.
Matthew 5:25-26:	Advice that it is best to make peace with an adversary who is taking you to court. Otherwise, a prison term may be forthcoming.
Matthew 11:2:	John the Baptist, who is in prison, asks Jesus if He is the One who was to come.
Matthew 14:3,10:	John the Baptist imprisoned and beheaded.
Matthew 18:30:	The unmerciful servant puts a man who owes him money into jail.
Matthew 25:35,39,44:	Jesus states that people who minister to those in prison are ministering to Him and that people who do not minister to those who are in prison have not ministered to Him.
Matthew 27:15-21:	Barabbas released by the crowds.
Mark 1:14; 6:17,27:	John the Baptist imprisoned and beheaded.
Mark 15:6:	Barabbas released from prison.
Luke 3:20:	John the Baptist imprisoned.
Luke 4:18:	Jesus states His calling, the fulfillment of Isaiah 61:1-3.
Luke 12:58-59:	Advice to reconcile yourself to your adversary so you might escape imprisonment.
Luke 21:12-13:	Jesus tells His disciples that they will be imprisoned on account of His name and that this would result in their being witnesses.
Luke 22:33:	Peter declares he is ready to follow Jesus to prison and death.
Luke 23:19,25:	The release of Barabbas at the request of the people.
Acts 4:3:	Peter and John imprisoned.

Acts 5:18-23:	The apostles imprisoned then freed by an angel of the Lord.
Acts 5:40:	The apostles beaten for preaching the name of Jesus.
Acts 7:54-60:	Stephen stoned to death.
Acts 8:3; 9:2,14,21:	Saul persecuting Christians, his conversion and his ministry.
Acts 12:1-2:	James, the brother of John, put to death by the sword at the command of Herod.
Acts 12:3-17:	Peter imprisoned and released by an angel of the Lord.
Acts 12:18-19:	Herod puts to death the guards who had been watching Peter.
Acts 14:19:	Paul stoned by the crowd and assumed dead.
Acts 16:25-39:	Paul and Silas beaten and imprisoned. An earthquake erupts, the prison doors fly open, the chains are loosed. The jailer accepts salvation and Paul and Silas are freed by the magistrates.
Acts 20:22-24:	Paul predicts his imprisonment in Jerusalem.
Acts 21:11:	Agabus, a prophet, confirms that Paul will be imprisoned in Jerusalem.
Acts 21:30-35:	The crowd in Jerusalem seizes Paul with the intention to kill him. Paul is saved by Roman soldiers.
Acts 22:24-29:	Paul testifies that he previously persecuted Christians.
Acts 23:1-35:	Paul speaks before the Sanhedrin and is imprisoned.
Acts chapter 24:	Paul's trial before Felix and his appeal to Ceasar.
Acts chapter 25:	Paul's trial before Festus.
Acts chapter 26:	Paul's trial before Agrippa.
Acts chapter 27:1-28:15:	Paul's trip to Rome while in custody of Roman soldiers.
Acts 28:17-20:	Paul talks about his imprisonment.
Acts 28:16:	Paul allowed to live in his own house with a guard to watch him.
Acts 28:17-20:	Paul talks about his imprisonment.

2 Corinthians 11:23:	Paul talks about his imprisonments and hardships he has suffered for Christ.
Ephesians 3:1; 4:1:	Paul states he is a prisoner of Christ.
Ephesians 6:20:	Paul states he is an ambassador in chains.
Philippians 1:11-18:	Paul states that his imprisonment has advanced the cause of Christ.
Colossians 4:10:	Aristarchus is a fellow prisoner of Paul.
2 Timothy 1:8:	Paul asks that people not be ashamed of his bondage in Christ.
2 Timothy 1:16-17:	Paul blesses Onesiphorus for his ministry to him in prison
2 Timothy 2:9:	Paul says that although he is bound, the Word of God is not bound
2 Timothy 4:16-17:	The Lord stood by Paul's side when everyone else deserted him because of his imprisonment
Philemon 1:9-10:	Paul requests mercy for Onesimus who was saved in prison.
Philemon 1:23:	Epaphras, a fellow prisoner of Paul.
Hebrews 13:3:	Remember those in prison as if you were their fellow prisoners.
1 Peter 3:19:	Christ ministers to those in prison
2 Peter 2:4:	God imprisoned the angels who revolted against Him
Jude 1:6:	God imprisoned the angels who revolted against Him.
Revelation 2:10:	The devil will imprison some in order to test them.
Revelation 2:13:	Antipas, God's faithful witness, put to death.
Revelation 20:7:	Satan released from prison for a short time.

CHAPTER FIVE

LEGAL AND ORGANIZATIONAL STRUCTURE OF YOUR MINISTRY

I have included this section to help those of you who are unable to start an ex-offender ministry within your church and wish to do it as a separate legal entity from the church itself. In most of the previous writing, I have written with the implication that many of you wish to start a ministry under the legal, spiritual, and organizational umbrella of your local church. In that case, you would probably not need to be worried about legal organization, since your church would be already set up as a legal entity, and your ministry would function under that entity. However, if you wish to start your ministry as a separate organization, you may wish to follow some of the tips I give below. It would be wise for you to obtain the advice of an attorney in your area, and to use the tips below only as general guidance.

GET THE LEGAL AND SPIRITUAL COVERING OF A LOCAL CHURCH

Setting up a new organization could take anywhere from 6 months to a little over a year, depending on your jurisdiction and the effort needed to meet all requirements. Getting your IRS tax-exempt status could take 6 months alone. If you want to receive donations before your ministry is officially tax-exempt, then you may wish to organize under the umbrella of a local church until your tax-exempt status is approved. Donors could then give to the church, and the donations could be earmarked for your ministry. Consult with an attorney to determine the specifics of this action.

Also, establishing a separate organization from the church does not mean that you should reject the spiritual covering of the church. Never, ever, establish a separate organization out of rebellion. Make it a point to seek out a pastor or a church that is willing to serve as the organization's spiritual covering. The pastor should be a member of your organization's board or Advisory Board. Since he is appointed and anointed by God to provide leadership in spiritual matters, he should be kept apprised of the goings-on in your ministry and given opportunity to speak wisdom before major decisions are made.

LEGAL FORM OF YOUR ORGANIZATION

First of all, the form of your organization should be a non-profit corporation. In most states, a corporation is an organization governed by a Board of Directors of at least 3 people and organized under a charter, or articles of incorporation, that must be filed with the state. For a corporation, the Board of Directors as a whole is the legal entity, not one or two individuals, as would be the case with a sole proprietorship or a partnership.

A non-profit corporation, then, is a corporation in which the profits of that corporation are funneled back into the corporation for funding of its programs. It is the counterpart of a business corporation, in which the organization's profits are distributed to shareholders. A non-profit corporation has no shareholders, no members that financially benefit from the organization. This does not mean that the non-profit organization cannot hire people. It can, although in some states there may be a limit on hiring Board members as staff. But in this case, the people hired must be performing services for the organization under the organization's control.

A non-profit organization provides an accountability structure and a system whereby most of the money handled by the organization is used for to further its mission. By its definition alone, this is the most attractive legal structure for most any ministry. Pursuing any other legal structure removes the accountability of a Board of Directors, and makes your ministry ineligible to receive contributions from other corporations, foundations, churches, and individuals, since many of them will give only if the organization is a non-profit corporation that is tax-exempt under the laws of the Internal Revenue Service.

Now, discussing all this legal stuff could take another 50 pages, so here's the deal. If you are starting a ministry outside your church, get some God-loving, God-fearing people who are mature, excellent organizers and are so excited about your mission for ex-offenders that they arer willing to serve as Board members and contribute some seed money to get the ministry started. Then, get a lawyer and an accountant (or two people who are familiar with the Federal and state laws and procedures for non-profit organizations), get everyone around a table and discuss the vision and mission of your organization, what you want to accomplish and how you want to accomplish it. When you are done, you should have a charter ready to submit to the regulatory agency in your state.

Do not treat this document lightly! Your charter will be the legal document describing your organization. Foundations will want to see your charter. Corporations will want to see it. You will be legally bound by what is in your charter. While many states will allow you to amend your charter, I recommend keeping your charter as nonspecific as possible, without being too vague. For instance, if your charter has a mission statement that reads:

Our organization is organized to help people.

That statement is too vague and indicates that you really did not know what you wanted to do when you started the organization. However, a statement that reads:

Our organization exists to serve people who are impoverished through no fault of their own.

This statement says a little more about what the organization is about, but says nothing about how the organization will accomplish this. Here is a better statement:

Our organization exists to serve people who are impoverished through no fault of their own, by providing skills training to give them access to better employment.

On the other hand, here is a statement that is probably not a good idea:

Our organization exists to serve female ex-offenders who are impoverished through no fault of their own, by providing skills training in Microsoft Word in a classroom setting to enable them to get better jobs.

This statement may accurately reflect what you want to do now, but does not make room for any growth. Suppose later you want to serve male ex-offenders, as well as female. You will have to have a meeting of your Board of Directors, and conduct a vote just to change one word! It is best to start off with a broad statement that accurately portrays the benefits that your organization will provide to the public, without going into too many details. Reserve that detail for your bylaws, which your lawyer can explain better than I can here.

Once you have developed your charter, bylaws, and other legal documents that are required in your state, you can file these documents with your state's regulatory agency, pay the appropriate fees and, viola, you're a corporation. But you're not home yet.

Once you are officially a corporation, call your local IRS office and get two forms; an SS-4 (Application for Employer Identification Number), and a Form 1023/1024 (Application for Recognition of Exemption). You will also need to call your state's tax office and find out what forms you need to file with them.

Form SS-4 is fairly easy and can be filled out without the assistance of an attorney. Form 1023/1024 is another story. I would strongly recommend getting a lawyer or accountant to help you, but if you are a do-it-yourselfer (as I am), here are a few tips. Remember, this form is very important. The information you put on this form determines whether you will be given recognition of exemption from income tax, which will determine whether donors can deduct the value of their gifts to you.

    a) Review the IRS Code applying to tax-exempt organizations.

b) Study the form carefully and answer every question completely and accurately.

c) Make sure you have sat down with your Board and come up with a strategic plan of action for your organization. The IRS will want to know about the hiring of employees, the compensation given to them, what your organization will do if a client cannot pay, job descriptions, where the money will come from, how you will get it, etc. It is best to have thought of these types of issues beforehand, because when the IRS asks for this information, they will want it within 3 weeks.

The filing of the Form 1023/1024 is not free. It will cost you hundreds of dollars. The Form 1023/1024 will detail the exact cost. Be prepared to pay it. This is where your seed money from your Board members will come in handy.

Prepare to wait anywhere from 3-9 months for a reply. However, the more accurate and complete your application, the quicker it will be.

Once you file your application for exemption, wait until you receive word from them about your tax-exempt status before receiving any donations directly. Once you receive such word, you can begin collecting donations and completing plans for your ministry.

For more information, I recommend the book, *A Nonprofit Organization and Operating Manual-Planning for Survival and Growth*, by Arnold J. Olenick and Philip R. Olenick, available from The Foundation Center, 79 Fifth Avenue, New York, NY 10003-3050.

CHAPTER SIX

STARTING AN AFTERCARE CENTER

In this section, I will suggest some general guidelines for starting an Aftercare center for ex-offenders. Some of these guidelines were implemented by the Board of Directors of Conquest Offender Reintegration Ministries in preparation for our future Aftercare Center here in Washington, DC. Some guidelines were culled from information obtained from visiting other successful Aftercare centers around the country, and from talking with professionals in community corrections.

The advantage of having an aftercare center is that ex-offenders are not forced to go to a shelter, or to an environment that could be damaging to them. They can come to a building that is Christian-run and functions according to Biblical principles. They can come to an environment that is conducive to personal and spiritual growth.

Let me define what an aftercare center is. It is a structured living environment that employs resources to help men and women struggling with crime to order their lives through Biblical discipleship and instruction. It is not a *halfway house (a community correctional center where inmates are sent to serve a portion of their sentence in the community)*. It is not a *homeless shelter (a place where homeless men and women can receive food, clothing, and shelter, usually overnight only)*. It is not a *drug and alcohol rehabilitation or treatment center (a medical facility that houses patients struggling with drug or alcohol abuse)*. It *is* a Christian home for former offenders, a home that has rules and regulations and a structured environment. Some of your clients may be homeless, others may be on parole, and others may be getting outpatient treatment for drug or alcohol abuse. But the purpose of the center should be to focus on Biblical training and personal and spiritual development in a live-in environment.

I will give some guidelines for starting and operating an aftercare center. But first, if you have skipped through this entire manual to get to this section, I would start from the beginning of this manual and read before going any further with this section. Many of the elements discussed elsewhere in this manual will need to be applied to your aftercare center ministry.

GETTING STARTED

Good ministry requires good government. One of the first things you need to do is develop a management structure for the center. When this center is developed, who is legally responsible for it? Who is spiritually responsible?

You will need to develop a Board that is responsible for governing the center. The Board can be organized as a separate corporation, or can be a committee or sub-board of another Board, such as your church Board. If it is a sub-board, then your church has ultimate responsibility. If it is an autonomous Board, then this Board has final authority (see developing a ministry team, above).

Once the Board is established, it should have several meetings toward the purpose of developing a paper describing the proposed center in flawless detail. Some of the questions that should be answered in this paper are:

1) How many people will we serve? How large should this center be?
2) Can our budget handle the increased expense? If not, how will we pay for it?
3) What types of offenders shall we serve?
4) Where should this center be located?
5) Are there any zoning restrictions? Are licenses required?
6) Does the community support this center?
7) Do we have outside resources available to handle areas we are not equipped to handle, such as medical needs?
8) Can we locate a good Director for the center?
9) What types of security should be in place? How much supervision shall we employ?
10) Do we have good relationships with parole officers in the community?
11) What rules and regulations shall we adopt?
12) What are the penalties for violating rules and regulations?
13) What is the procedure for hearing grievances?
14) What should the typical resident's schedule be?
15) Should we charge rent?
16) What types of in-house services should we offer?
17) How long should a typical stay at the center be?

As an example, I have included in the appendix pertinent sections of our Transitional Housing Center Operations Manual. These guidelines answer the questions above and are intended to illustrate the types of planning and thinking that must go into your Center.

CHAPTER SEVEN

THE HARVEST

I have often said that ministering to ex-offenders can prepare you for any other type of ministry. Ex-offenders often carry with them the same types of problems as the rest of society. The only difference is, somewhere along the line, they got caught and were sent to prison. Criminals and sociopaths are broad, unfair terms to describe them. They are real people with real problems. They are people, like you and I, who have been pushed to the brink. They are persons who have much in common with the rest of us, but have been deceived into thinking that crime was the answer. Judging by the number of Scriptures dealing with prisoners, they are on the heart of God.

God is open doors for the next round of faithful men and women that will go into the streets and into the prisons and set the captives free. He is preparing to bring men and women out of prison and to prepare them for the work that He would have them to do. The demographics of God's army is composed of people like ex-offenders who have been to the depths of despair and hopelessness and, with the Lord's strong hand, have surfaced with a mighty testimony of the Lord's grace. Out there, right now, is a harvest ripe for the plucking. It is in America's prisons and jails, and in prisons and jails all over the world. The church, if it wants to be serious about saving souls, can not ignore those who have been guilty of wrongdoing. After all, the greatest act of justice in the world happened on that hill on Calvary, when Jesus Christ gave His life so that we all could have remission of sins. He loved us so, that He looked beyond our faults, and saw our needs. He gave His life, that you and I could have our sins forgiven and have a new life in Christ. This is what Jesus Christ did for you and me.

Offering that same grace to ex-offenders is the least we can do in return. God bless you as you pray and ask the Lord to strengthen you, keep you and guide you in consideration of this very important work.

APPENDIX

OTHER RESOURCES

BENEFITS FOR THE ELDERLY AND DISABLED

Persons that are medically disabled and/or over 62 years of age may benefit from your knowledge about the resources from the Social Security Administration. There are three basic benefits that you can receive from the Federal government. Contact your local Social Security Administration office or your local welfare or social services office for more information and application procedures.

Social Security
This type of benefit, commonly know as Social Security, is actually called Old Age, Survivors and Disability Insurance (OASDI) This "government pension plan" is available to persons 62 years of age and over who have made contributions to social security through payroll deduction. The amount of Social Security you get is based upon how much you have paid into the program at the time you receive benefits. This program has provisions for children, spouses, and survivors of those earning Social Security benefits. If you have clients who are age 62 and over, you will want to explore the benefits of this program.

Social Security Disability Insurance Benefits (SSDIB)
Persons who are not yet 62 years of age, but otherwise qualify for Social Security, may be eligible for these benefits if they are unable to work for health reasons.

Supplemental Security Income (SSI)
SSI is a federal welfare program for adults and children with disabilities and persons over 65 years of age who have low income and few financial resources. SSI does not require you to qualify for Social Security, and you may be able to receive SSI and Social Security benefits at the same time.

Medicare
This is a national health insurance policy for senior citizens and people with disabilities. Persons 65 years of age and over may qualify for this program, regardless of income. Medicare Part A is the hospitalization insurance component of the program. It carries a deductible. A co-payment also kicks in if you are in the hospital more than 60 days. Medicare Part B is the medical insurance component, which covers most outpatient care. A low monthly premium is usually charged for this service. There are also insurance policies available from private insurance companies that will pay for deductibles and co-payments left over from from Medicare.

Medicaid
People who are low income, with few assets, and who are eligible to receive other public

assistance benefits such as SSI may be eligible for this program that covers some medical expenses, depending upon the state. They may be a charge for Medicaid, and the qualification procedures are very complex.

THE WORK OPPORTUNITY TAX CREDIT ACT

This is a tax credit that can be claimed on an employer's federal tax return for hiring low income ex-offenders. This credit, 35% of the first $6000 of wages paid to an eligible employee, is an added incentive for employers to hire ex-offenders. The required paperwork for applying for the tax credit and more information can be obtained by calling the WOTC Program at 303-620-4224. This credit was slated to expire for all workers hired after December 2001.

FEDERAL AND STATE BONDING FOR EX-OFFENDERS

The Federal government and some state government have fidelity bonding available for ex-offenders. Fidelity bonding is insurance made available to the ex-offender and covers the employer in case of theft or dishonesty on the part of the ex-offender. This bonding program is made available because of the reluctance of commercial bonding programs to provide bonding to ex-offenders based on their backgrounds.

More information on the Federal Bonding program can be obtained by writing or calling your state employment agency, or by writing the Federal Bonding Program, 1725 DeSales Street N.W. Suite 900, Washington, D.C. 20036. Their telephone number is 202-293-5566 or 800-233-2258.

INTERNATIONAL UNION OF GOSPEL MISSIONS

This is a union of 272 member ministries that operates programs around the country that are relevant to ex-offenders. The member ministries operate traditional rescue mission programs including overnight shelter, food, etc., while others operate non-traditional programs such as rehabilitation programs, community outreach ministries, Women and Family Ministries, urban youth ministry, alcohol-drug support group network, jail ministry, and soup kitchen.

1045 Swift Street
Kansas City, MO 64116-4127 USA
Phone: (816) 471-8020
FAX (816)471-3718

TEEN CHALLENGE

Teen Challenge is the oldest, largest and most successful program of its kind in the world. Established in 1958 by David Wilkerson, Teen Challenge has grown to more than 120 centers in the United States and 250 centers world-wide. Teen Challenge offers a number of services to the community, many times free of charge. Teen Challenge reaches out to people in juvenile halls, jails, and prisons. Their "jail teams" help show inmates that their is hope for them to turn their lives around.

P.O. Box 745

Locust Grove, VA 22508
TEL: (540) 972-8223
Fax: (540) 972-8424
E-MAIL:tciworld@flash.net

REENTRY JAIL AND PRISON MINISTRY

This excellent web site, run by Chaplain Art Lyons, contains a state-by-state listing of resources for prison ministry and post-prison ministry. The site can be accessed by pointing your web browser to http://www.reentry.org. Chaplain Lyons also has published a book that contains much of the same resources contained in his web site.

NATIONAL PRISON MINISTRIES

The national prison ministries listed below have a great deal of resources available for ministries to inmates and ex-offenders. These resources include publications, training programs, and outreaches to inmates, ex-offenders, and their families.

International Prison Ministry
Box 63
Dallas, TX 75221
800-527-1212
Makes available Bibles, books, and tracts to inmates and prison ministries nationwide.

Prison Fellowship Ministries
P.O. Box 17500
Washington, DC 20041-0500
703-478-0100
An international family of ministries founded in 1976 by former Nixon aide Chuck Colson. Prison Fellowship has several ministries that work with inmates, ex-offenders, families of offenders, and crime victims. To find out what Prison Fellowship is doing with ex-offenders in your community, call the above number and ask for the number of the local office serving your area..

Bill Glass Ministries
P.O. Box 900
Cedar Hill, TX 75106-2349
972-291-7895
Based in Cedar Hill, TX, this evangelical ministry exists to evangelize cities, schools, and prisons around the nation with its Prison Evangelism, City-Wide Celebrations, and Youth Outreach programs.

KAIROS Prison Ministry
140 N. Orlando Ave. Suite 180
Winter Park, FL 32789-3680
407-629-4948
This organization builds strong Christian communities in prisons by establishing and leading

weekly share and prayer groups of inmates.

COPE (Coalition of Prison Evangelists)
2220 Regal Parkway
Euless, TX 76040
1-888-ALO-COPE

COPE is a professional service organization for Christians ministering in the field of Corrections. COPE is a network of over 550 jail and prison ministries throughout the country and the world, sharing resources and services. Some of the services that COPE provides each of its member ministries includes the COPE Membership Directory listing every state & federal prison in the United States & Canada, their address & phone number, plus the name of the chaplain, plus every COPE ministry by state, the cooperating churches, a national list of traveling evangelists, music & singing groups, plus a nationwide list of aftercare residential centers for released prisoners.

Family and Corrections Network
32 Oak Grove Road
Palmyra, VA 22963
804-589-3036

This organization focuses on issues concerning families of offenders. They offer information on children of prisoners, parenting programs for prisoners, prison visiting, incarcerated fathers and mothers, hospitality, programs, prison marriage and more.

CONQUESTHOUSE TRANSITIONAL HOUSING FOR EX-OFFENDERS OPERATIONS MANUAL

Note: *This document is included with this manual to give you an idea of the structure and scope of our transitional aftercare outreach here in D.C. You may copy or adapt this manual and apply it to your own ministry.*

The following document details the operation and guidelines of our Discipleship Center. Every resident must read, understand and agree to all of these guidelines, and must sign a Memorandum of Understanding to this effect. All volunteers, mentors, employees, Board members, committee members and anyone else having an interest in the Discipleship Center must read and understand these guidelines. This document is to be considered as the official policy and operations guide of the Discipleship Center, and has been developed with every consideration for the well-being of the residents, the staff and employees of ConquestHouse, and the neighborhood in which the Discipleship Center is located.

PURPOSE OF THE DISCIPLESHIP CENTER

The Discipleship Center Project will serve homeless ex-offenders by providing transitional housing and several support services, including case management, job training and placement services, and Biblical discipleship through volunteer mentors. The Discipleship Center Project will help provide its residents with the resources they need to become productive citizens and to reintegrate themselves into the community without reverting to self-destructive patterns of behavior.

Project goals and objectives are as follows:

Meeting Immediate Needs
Provision of transitional shelter, food, clothing.
Obtain employment or enroll in job training programs

Education
Develop or strengthen ability to read and write
Improve ability to budget and deal with finances
Cultivate basic life skills
Encourage enrollment in courses to strengthen ability to obtain a better job, such as computer or trade courses.

Social and Spiritual Reintegration
Disciple residents into Christian maturity
Nurture desire to volunteer and serve to better the community.
Develop skills in conflict resolution and anger control.
Improve ability to deal with stress or adverse situations.
Renew and/or strengthen quality relationships with family and community.
Graft the individual into a local church body.
Cultivate moral values and responsibility.

Economic Empowerment
Develop budgeting and controlled spending habits
Maintain a savings account
Encourage good work habits and a positive work ethic

The Center will also be an agent to improve public safety and increase the public's confidence in ex-offenders by:

a) producing men and women who are empowered morally, socially, physically and spiritually, and:

b) eventually releasing these men and women into the community to make a positive contribution by helping and supporting others like themselves.

HOW THIS PROGRAM BENEFITS ITS RESIDENTS AND ITS COMMUNITY

Statistics indicate that 60-75% of the inmates released from prison will return for either a parole violation or a new offense within three years. Statistics also show that when these offenders are offered programs that combine Christian teaching and discipleship with mentoring, job training, transitional housing, and other support services, the recidivism rate drops dramatically. Many ex-offenders are mal-adjusted to society, having to deal with the stigma that comes with being an ex-offender, in addition to his own personal struggles and habits that lead to criminal behavior in the first place. Crime is ultimately an action of the heart. Rehabilitation in today's prisons is almost non-existent, reduced to a few scattered programs in a few prisons that do nothing to change the human heart. Religious based programs have been shown to reach the human heart in such a way that it infuses hope, makes the offender feel better about himself, gives the ex-offender a purpose for living, and introduces him to a God that is more powerful than himself, allowing him the privilege of "partnering" with someone who can provide deliverance through any struggle.

A basic tenet of Christianity is that all mankind, regardless of how good they are, how pious they think they are, or how many good deeds they have done, is sinful. It is a condition brought on by the willful transgression of Adam in the Garden of Eden. The Scripture says that through Adam, all mankind has sinned, but through Christ, all mankind has been made alive. The fact that all mankind has sinned and offended the Father places each of us, man, woman, and child, in need of salvation. For the Bible says that the wages of sin is death, but the gift of God is eternal life through Jesus Christ our Lord. Jesus Christ, through his love and mercy, and because of his death on the cross, allows all sinners to be restored to God through faith in Him. Jesus Christ' substitutionary sacrifice on the cross at Calvary is the greatest act of mercy mankind has ever been offered. No sin can be greater than the sin of offending the Father. And all of us have done just that.

Having receiving God's mercy through His precious son, Jesus Christ, and having been saved from our sins through faith in Him and obedience to His word, the members of ConquestHouse now demonstrate his love and mercy through this program designed to help those who have sinned not only against God, but against mankind. Because we have received mercy, we extend mercy to others, in Jesus' name. We recognize that if it were not for the mercies of God, we would be doomed to a live of sin and separation from God.

Our program employs Biblical discipleship, which is the process of mentoring individuals to a fuller and deeper relationship with the Lord Jesus Christ. It connects ex-offenders to their life source, and causes them to rely upon Christ rather than on their own feelings, attitudes or actions. It reduces crime by helping to reduce the importance and impact of material things, attitudes, and addictions, and causes ex-offenders to depend solely upon the blessing and mercies of Jesus Christ. It, in effect, takes the ex-offender out of the world's method of operation, and into the Bible's method of operation. Since the Bible is anti-crime, those that adhere to the Bible's teachings will also become anti-crime, and eventually, will even join efforts to stop others from doing the same crimes that they did. This is the beauty of the Gospel.

This program also prevents homelessness and puts ex-offenders in a positive Christian environment. Ex-offenders who enter this program and complete it successfully will return to society as changed men, determined to be law-abiding and determined to help others do the same.

GOVERNMENT OF THE PROGRAM

All Discipleship Center activities will be managed by the Board of Directors of ConquestHouse, Inc. The Board of Directors, at its discretion, may nominate and appoint members of a committee to provide direct oversight to the Discipleship Center; including the evaluation, screening, and selection of residents, provided that the committee consists of at least two Board members. The committee will report to the Board of Directors on all issues related to the

Discipleship Center.

The Board of Directors shall also appoint a Program Director. The Program Director will provide day-to-day administration of the Discipleship Center, and shall be a member of the governing committee, if established by the Board. The Program Director shall also be responsible for hiring support staff necessary for the daily operation of the Center (see Appendix for list of support staff).

The Program Director shall appoint a Resident Director. The Resident Director shall be responsible for implementing the policies and procedures detailed in this manual under the supervision of the Program Director. The Resident Director will reside full-time in the dwelling where the Discipleship Center Program is located.

All grievances related to the operation of the Discipleship Center should be relayed to the Program Director. If the appeal to the Program Director does not bring satisfactory resolution, then the grievance should be addressed in writing to the Discipleship Center committee. If the committee does not bring satisfactory resolution, then the appeal should be addressed in writing to the Board of Directors. The Board of Directors will make the final point of appeal for all grievances for which it is legally responsible.

DURATION OF THE PROGRAM

Generally, all residents will remain in the program for a period of no less than six months and no more than one year. An extension of up to one year may be granted by the Board of Directors if special circumstances warrant an additional stay. These circumstances include:

a) Illness, injury or disability, other than those that are self-inflicted, that delays the resident's development and participation in the program.
b) Layoff or other involuntary termination of employment (not including termination for cause) within one month of the resident's date for leaving the program.
c) Any other hardship out of the resident's control that would cause

the resident to be significantly at risk of homelessness if he/she were to leave the program at the scheduled time.

PAYMENT FOR SERVICES

Program Payment
ConquestHouse will expect each resident of the Discipleship Center to contribute $300.00 monthly as a program payment. This payment will be due on the first of the month following the month in which the resident becomes gainfully employed for three weeks, and every first of the month thereafter until the resident leaves the program. This payment not only helps the Discipleship Center meet its expenses, but helps the resident immediately start to budget and become accustomed to a regular schedule of paying rent and financial responsibility. No other payments or other compensation are expected of the residents. Residents are expected to put aside 5-10 percent of their gross monthly earnings into an escrow account managed by ConquestHouse. When the resident leaves the facility, the money in the resident's escrow account (minus any unpaid program payments) will be returned to the resident as a nest egg to help the resident with security deposit, first month's rent, and other moving expenses.

Receipts for payment and account logs
Any money tendered by residents to ConquestHouse, whether for program payments or for escrow account savings, shall be recorded in an account log. This log shall be made a part of the resident's file. The resident shall have the right to receive a copy of their account log anytime during normal business hours.

Residents shall also be issued a receipt for each payment made to ConquestHouse, whether for program payments, escrow account savings, or any other payment for any reason.

Failure to Pay Program Payment
If the resident fails to pay program payment in accordance with the above paragraph, by the fifth of the month in which it is due, the resident will receive a written notice informing him that payment is due, the amount of the payment, and that refusal to tender payment within 5 days of the notice may result in dismissal from the program.

This notice shall be called a "Five Day Notice", and shall be the only written notification given to residents about rent arrears. If the resident pays within the five day period, the Five Day Notice shall be cancelled, and the resident shall be allowed to remain in the program. If the Resident does not pay within the Five Day period prescribed by the Notice, the Resident, at the discretion of the Board of Directors, shall be subjected to Probationary Termination, as outlined below.

DEPARTURE FROM THE PROGRAM

A resident may voluntarily depart from the program at any time. However, we have determined that in order for the resident to gain the most benefit from the program, he/she needs to invest at least six months of time into the program. If a resident chooses to depart, any property or monies belonging to the resident which are in the possession of ConquestHouse shall be returned to the resident (minus any unpaid rent) immediately upon leaving the premises. Money shall be returned via company check (no cash). All property left on the premises once the resident departs the premises shall be considered to be the property of ConquestHouse.

Two types of terminations may be initiated by the Board of Directors of ConquestHouse. They are:
   a) Probationary termination
   b) Termination for cause

Probationary termination
A resident may be given a probationary termination by majority vote of the Discipleship Committee or the Board of Directors if the Discipleship Committee or the Board of Directors feels for any reason that the resident should not continue in the program. A probationary termination will be issued to the resident in writing, with a copy being issued to the resident's mentors or church family. Probationary terminations are effective 30 calendar days from the date of issue. All benefits from the program remain in effect during this period. Upon expiration of 30 days from the date of notice issue, the resident will be expected to leave the program, and all program benefits will cease.

Termination for cause

A resident may also be terminated for cause by a majority vote of the Discipleship Committee, or the Board of Directors, in writing, for any the following reasons:

a) misconduct, including violation of program rules and violation of the law.
b) proving false information on admissions application.
c) Any other action, behavior or thoughts on the part of the resident which are determined to be detrimental or potentially detrimental to the health, safety or welfare of the other residents, ConquestHouse staff, or the community.

Terminations from the program for cause shall be immediate, and all benefits from the program shall immediately cease (This does not apply to any benefits the resident's family is receiving as a result of the resident's participation into the program, unless it is determined that the family was a knowing and willing party to the violation that caused the resident's dismissal).

Before any termination is given however, attempts by the Board of Directors shall be made to determine the nature of the violation and the circumstances behind it. The Board shall then make a decision based upon the evidence available.

Disposition of monies held in escrow account

All properties and monies belonging to the resident, terminated under either probationary termination or termination for cause, which are in the possession of ConquestHouse shall be returned to the resident (minus any unpaid rent) immediately upon termination. Money shall be returned via company check (no cash). All property left on the premises once the resident departs the premises shall be considered to be the property of ConquestHouse.

ENTRY INTO THE PROGRAM

An inmate or ex-offender wishing to stay at the Discipleship Center must be referred by either of the following persons:

a) A chaplain or pastor
b) A caseworker, social worker or warden
c) A prison minister or prison ministry program
d) A parole officer

The prisoner will complete an extensive application, which will then be signed by the referring official. The application is designed to get as much information about the applicant as we can.

Once the application is completed, the Discipleship Committee will review the application to determine if the applicant would be an appropriate candidate. At this point, background checks and criminal history checks will be conducted, and all references will be confirmed. If the applicant passes this stage, two or three members of the Discipleship committee will then go into the prison and interview the candidate. Based on the interview and all other information collected during the screening process, the Discipleship Committee will then make a decision as to whether or not the applicant will be admitted into the program. The Board of Directors, however, must approve the decision of the Discipleship Committee before informing the applicant.

Applicant Qualifications
In any case, the applicant must meet the following criteria in order to be accepted:

1) Must have been incarcerated for more than 6 months in a correctional facility and must be approved to reside in the Washington, DC area after release.
2) Must not be under the supervision of any DC Department of Corrections agency.
3) Must be able physically and mentally to sustain employment.
4) Income should not exceed the poverty levels established by DHHS. In determining what constitutes as income, ConquestHouse will consider all funds made either through employment, welfare, government assistance, bequests and gifts, etc.
5) Must be a male age 18 or over
6) Be willing to submit to routine drug & AIDS screenings

7) Be homeless or in danger or being homeless upon release.
8) Must be a practicing Christian who either subscribes to the statement of faith included in this manual, or submits his own similar statement of faith.

If applicant is not selected

If an applicant is not selected for the program, the chaplain, prison ministry worker or social worker will be notified first, then the applicant, both in writing.

If applicant is selected

If the applicant is selected, the chaplain, prison ministry worker or social worker is notified, then the applicant is notified, both in writing. At this point, the rules of the program should be reviewed again with the applicant, and everything clearly understood. At this point, the applicant is considered to be an enrollee in the program, even though he has not officially entered the Discipleship Center yet.

ONE CHURCH ONE RESIDENT MENTORING

Once the applicant has been selected, ConquestHouse must immediately begin the process of selecting a church family that will "adopt" and mentor the resident throughout the duration of the program and beyond. ConquestHouse will work to develop and maintain relationships with Christian, Bible-believing churches in the Washington metropolitan area. These churches will "adopt" one resident of the Discipleship Center program. The adoption period will begin soon after selection. The church's responsibility to ConquestHouse and to the resident under OCOR shall be as follows:

a) To recruit volunteers who will serve as mentors to Christian residents during their stay in the program. The church will also become a spiritual family to the resident, and shall involve the resident in activities that are designed to make him/her feel a part of the family of fellowship.

b) The church should make every attempt possible to help pay for the resident's personal needs during the first 60 days of the program, and to help the resident gain employment. However, no money should be given directly to the resident.

It should be given to the Discipleship Center as a charitable contribution. The money will be allocated to pay for the resident's personal needs.

c) Mentors should be men or women that are spiritually mature and under the authority of the local church pastor or shepherd (see attached mentor qualifications). They are responsible for meeting with the resident at least once per week, for the purpose of counseling, Bible study, discipleship training, budgeting and prayer. Resident will be paired with mentors of the same sex.

d) The church is responsible for arranging transportation to and from church activities

e) The church is responsible for arranging dinner for the resident with a church family each Sunday.

f) The church shall inform ConquestHouse of any activities that would interfere with the resident's normal schedule at the Discipleship Center (see schedule in Appendix).

DISCIPLESHIP CENTER RULES AND REGULATIONS

It is important to the success of the program and to the rehabilitation of the resident to have a Center that is clean, well-managed, well-run and indicative of a Christian environment. Therefore, we insist on the following rules and regulations as a Code of Conduct during the resident's stay in the Discipleship Center. Violation of any of these rules may result in immediate dismissal.

These guidelines, with scriptural references, have been developed to cover most of the expectations we have for the residents at the Discipleship Center. A copy of these guidelines must be signed by each resident before entering the program.

1. Substance abuse of any nature is not permitted. A violation in or outside of the house is cause for termination of your residency. Notify the staff if you use prescription medications. (Proverbs 20:1, 1 Corinthians 3:16)
2. Smoking anywhere is not allowed. (1 Corinthians 6:12, 19-20)

3. Possession of weapons of any nature will terminate your residency. (Romans 8:56)
4. Residents shall be respectful of the property of other residents. Borrowing or trading is neither recommended nor advised. (Proverbs 22:7)
5. Residents shall attend and be on time for all required family, spiritual and financial meetings inside or away from the Discipleship Center, unless given prior permission by the Director.
6. Gambling or playing the lottery is not allowed. (Hebrews 13:5)
7. Residents shall treat other residents with consideration. Fights, threats, or aggressive behavior is not permitted in the house. Additionally, residents shall show respect for the staff, volunteers, visitors and Board members of ConquestHouse. (Romans 12:18)
8. Residents shall not engage in illicit sexual activity within the house. (1 Corinthians 6:13, Hebrews 12:16). Illicit sexual activity is defined as sexual relations or sexual touching with anyone other than your marital partner.
9. Borrowing or lending of money is not allowed between residents or between residents and staff. The Director should approve, in advance, the lending or borrowing of money between the resident and someone outside of the house. (Proverbs 22:7)
10. Being truthful and above board about everything during your stay at the Discipleship Center is expected. (Proverbs 12:22)
11. Residents must notify the Director when they plan to be away from the Center. This is for the resident's protection and is part of being a responsible and accountable family member. Name address and phone number of employer, supervisor, pay period, and work schedule of each resident shall be maintained on file by the Director. (1 Peter 2:13a, 17c)
12. Consistent fellowship in an approved church and fellowship and discipleship with a mentor will help each resident build continued self-confidence, lessen negative temptations, and provide encouragement during a resident's stay at the Discipleship Center. Church attendance and the mentor relationship will also prepare them to live independently from the Center. (Hebrews 10:24-25)
13. Each resident shall cooperate with the other residents to keep the house clean. Beds shall be made, dirty clothes shall be picked-up, bathroom cleaned, dishes washed, and garbage taken out. Resident rooms shall be presentable at all times. All appliances

shall be turned off when not in use. (Ecclesiastics 9:10; Proverbs 10:4)
14. Personal hygiene, clean clothes, and general household cleanliness *are very* important and expected form each resident. Appropriate attire shall be worn at all times.
15. In consideration of others, residents shall keep noise levels down and activities to a minimum during quiet times as listed in the Schedule of Activities. Residents are commanded to adhere to the schedule listed in the Schedule of Activities. Building will be locked during curfew hours, and no entry or exit from the building will be permitted except in the case of an emergency. (James 3:17-18)
16. The first month of residency is without program payment. The first month of the program is probationary. Residency can be terminated for any reason 30 days after the probationary period.
17. Casual and personal visitors are allowed in the Center only during free time periods. Visitors must remain in common areas, and shall not be allowed in the residents' rooms. Business visitors (defined as professional persons assisting the resident with employment, legal, medical, financial, and spiritual issues), shall be allowed in the Center during free times and during the hours of 7:00 am – 5:00 pm Monday through Friday, unless an emergency exists. ConquestHouse employees, Board members, advisory committee members, and mentors may enter the building at any time. Other ConquestHouse volunteers may access the building during any non-curfew hour.
18. These rules may be amended or added to with Policy Memorandums developed by the Board of Directors, or by the Director in consultation with the Board. Each Policy Memorandum developed should be considered as an integral part of these rules and regulations, and should be listed under the document list on the front of this manual. Any change in the policies, rules and regulations listed here should be made via Policy Memorandum, and a copy given to each exiting resident and all staff and volunteers. The resident must sign a copy of the Policy Memorandum and return it to the Director for inclusion in the resident's file. From that point, the resident will be expected to adhere to the Policy Memorandum.

COVERAGE FOR RESIDENT DIRECTOR IN CASE

OF ABSENCE

Should the Resident Director, for any reason, become unable to perform his duties, or cannot remain in the building during any of the on-premises hours posted in the schedule, the Program Director shall become the Resident Director and shall assume all responsibilities and privileges of the Resident Director during the period when the Resident Director cannot perform his duties. In lieu of this, the Program Director shall immediately appoint someone to serve as an interim Resident Director until either a new Resident Director is hired, or the existing Resident Director is able to perform his duties as scheduled. Any person serving as interim Resident Director must meet the same qualifications as detailed in the Resident Director job description.

MEALS AND FOOD PREPARATION

ConquestHouse shall make available to all residents three meals per day, in accordance with DCMR Title 22. No charge shall be expected for meals. The resident may, at his discretion, purchase his own meals. ConquestHouse shall not be responsible for any meals the resident purchases on his own accord, except to provide adequate and reasonable storage.

RULES FOR SAFETY AND CLEANLINESS

While residents will contribute to the cleanliness and safety of the house, it is ultimately the Resident Director's responsibility to ensure that the house is safe, clean and sanitary in accordance with DCMR Title 22. Consequently, the following procedures have been instituted.

1) All bed coverings, dish cloths, bathroom towels, wash cloths, and table cloths must be changed at least once per week. Resident Director shall create a schedule to help manage changing of the linens. Changing the linens shall be the responsibility of the Resident Director. No linens shall be put into any use in the house unless they have been thoroughly cleansed using laundry

detergent and hot water, and dried thoroughly. Cleaned linens should be stored indoors in an area free from dust, moisture or food products. Unclean linens shall be placed in a container and stored away from any resident's room, bathroom or kitchen.

2) All bathtubs and showers should be cleansed with scouring powder or an approved cleanser after each use. All toilets should be thoroughly cleansed with a disinfectant at least once per week, or often if needed. Toilet seats should be cleaned and disinfected immediately if feces or urine comes in contact with them. Bathroom sinks should be cleaned at least once per day. Floors and surfaces in the bathrooms should be cleaned and disinfected at least four times per week. Floors, sinks and food preparation surfaces in kitchens should be cleaned and disinfected after each instance of food preparation.

3) Rubbish and refuse shall be removed from the premises at least once per day. Rubbish and refuse shall be placed in approved containers outside of the building. Rubbish containers shall be emptied at least once per week by a trash removal contractor.

4) Each room in the building shall be serviced by an exterminator at least once per month.

5) All cracks and crevices leading from the outside to the inside of the building shall be plugged to prevent entry of vermin and other pests.

6) All hardwood or tile floors, other than those in the kitchens and bathrooms, shall be swept and/or vacuumed and mopped at least once per week. All carpeted floors shall be vacuumed at least once per week.

7) All windows should have screens affixed to them to prevent insects from entering the building. No window without a screen should be open, unless it is just for a few minutes.

8) All food and food products, unless they are being consumed, should be stored in covered plastic, glass or metal containers and

placed in appropriate storage places. No food should be left in rooms uncovered. No food shall be allowed in bathrooms.

9) All residents should be given fire exit instructions.

10) Residents shall be allowed access to a washer and dryer during non-curfew hours and shall be responsible for their own laundry, with the exception of linens.

11) Residents shall be responsible for their own personal effects, including clothes, body products, toothbrushes, toothpaste, hair products, grooming products, etc. Bathroom soap and kitchen products shall be provided by ConquestHouse.

12) No pets will be allowed on the premises.

13) ConquestHouse shall arrange for the proper and secure storage of prescription medicines for each resident.

14) ConquestHouse shall provide a lockable storage cabinet for each resident.

15) ConquestHouse shall ensure that all fire extinguishers, smoke detectors and fire alarms are in safe and working order, and that each resident, staff member, volunteer, Board member, and committee member knows the location of these devices.

16) ConquestHouse shall not block any window or door such that the resident cannot easily exit the building in case of emergency. This does not prevent ConquestHouse from installing an appropriate security system in order to keep intruders out of the building.

17) All stairs, hallways, and common areas should be kept free of all debris, including clothes, shoes, and other objects that could cause someone to trip and fall.

18) At least once per month, curtains, windows, and walls should be cleaned.

19) All Stairways, hallways, and walkways should be adequately lighted. Emergency lighting shall be installed in these areas in case of power failure.

20) Information concerning police, emergency medical services and hospitals, and EMS services, including 911, should be posted in a conspicuous place.

21) Residents shall not admit anyone other than residents to the premises unless that person or persons has been cleared through the Resident Director. Exceptions are as follows:

   a) Program mentors with identification
   b) Approved volunteers with identification
   c) Officials of the DC Department of Health, the DC Department of Consumer and Regulatory Affairs, the DC Fire Department, the DC Police Department, or any law enforcement agency in the process of conducting official business.
   d) Any person or persons holding a warrant to search or inspect the premises.

22) The grounds outside of the premises shall be kept clean and orderly. Grass should be cut on a regular basis. The grounds should be kept free of trash.

23) All additions and subtractions to these safety and cleanliness procedures shall be included in a policy Memorandum and attached to this manual.

CONQUESTHOUSE, INC. PERSONNEL

Following are the job descriptions for all of the program staff and contractors who will administer the Discipleship Center Program on a daily basis. In addition to the qualifications listed below, all applicants must be members of and accountable to a church located in the Washington, D.C. metropolitan area.

PROGRAM DIRECTOR

Full-Time, Permanent Position, 8 hrs./day, 5 days/week
The Program Director shall be the chief program officer and manager of the Corporation. The Program Director will operate the Corporation in all its activities and departments. The authority and responsibilities of the chief program officer shall include:

a. Carrying out all policies established by the Board of Directors and advising on the formation of these policies.
b. Developing and submitting to the Board of Directors for approval a plan of organization for the conduct of Corporate operation and recommending changes when necessary.
c. Preparing an annual budget showing the expected revenue and expenditures as required by the Board of Directors through its Budget Committee.
d. Selecting, employing, controlling, and discharging employees and developing and maintaining personnel policies and practices for the Corporation.
e. Maintaining physical properties in a good and safe state of repair and operating condition.
f. Supervising business affairs to ensure that funds are collected and expended to the best possible advantage.
g. Presenting to the Board of Directors, or its authorized committee, periodic reports reflecting the professional services and financial activities of the Corporation and such special reports as may be required by the Board of Directors.
h. Attending all meetings of the Board of Directors and serving on committees thereof.
i. Serving as the liaison and channel of communications between the Board of Directors and any of its committees.
j. Preparing a plan for the achievement of the Corporation's specific objectives and periodically reviewing and evaluating that plan.
k. Representing the Corporation in its relationships with other religious, voluntary or governmental agencies.
l. Performing other duties that may be necessary or in the best interest of the Corporation.

QUALIFICATIONS FOR POSITION:
Applicant must be a proven leader, must work well with others, must

be able to work without supervision, and have some experience working with inmates and ex-offenders and their families. At least two years of management or supervisory experience required. Must be skilled in crisis intervention. Security clearance required. High school diploma required. At least two years of college or other post-secondary training a strong plus.

ADMINISTRATIVE ASSISTANT
Full-Time, Permanent Position, 8 hrs./day, 5 days/week
The Administrative Assistant will act as the support of the ConquestHouse staff and will be responsible for assisting the Program Director. Responsibilities will include coordinating all day-to-day services of ConquestHouse, with the assistance of the resident manager, under the authority of the Program Director, as well as providing records administration, bookkeeping and secretarial support.

QUALIFICATIONS FOR POSITION:
Applicant must work well with others, have a pleasant telephone manner, possess excellent customer service skills and must be able to work without supervision. H.S. diploma and at least one year of office and bookkeeping experience required. Must be familiar with computer systems including software such as MS-DOS and Windows. Security clearance required.

RESIDENT DIRECTOR
Full-Time, live-in, Permanent Position
The Resident Director will be responsible for ensuring the day-to-day operation, upkeep and maintenance of the Discipleship Center and for obtaining the necessary contracted labor for maintaining the physical properties. The Resident Director will also interface with tenants as needed and be responsible for supervising and monitoring their day-to-day activities. The Resident Director will be available to respond to emergencies and to provide leadership in the absence of the Administrative Assistant and the Program Director. The Resident Director must reside full-time on the Discipleship Center premises and should be available during the hours set forth in the Discipleship Schedule of Activities. The Resident Director position is also a ministry position, requiring him to be able to minister to the residents

in spiritual matters.

QUALIFICATIONS FOR POSITION:

Applicant must be a proven leader, a Christian, must work well with others, must be able to work without supervision, and have some experience working with inmates and ex-offenders and their families. Some custodial or janitorial experience a plus, but not necessary. Must be skilled in crisis intervention. Security clearance required. High school diploma required. Must be healthy and free from communicable diseases. Pastor's recommendation required. Since this is a live-in position in a building that will not have accommodations for children, applicant should not have custody of any minor children.

CASE MANAGER
Contracted, 8 hours per week

The case manager will be responsible for meeting with residents and mentors and ensuring that residents receive appropriate social and health services. The case manager will identify services and resources in the community and will ensure that residents are referred to those services, according to their individual need. The case manager will also be responsible for making sure that each resident's file contains all documents required by center policy and by Federal and D.C. statute.

QUALIFICATIONS FOR POSITION

Associate or Bachelor's degree in a related field, and at least three years experience working with disadvantaged populations in a social work setting.

CULINARY SUPERVISOR
Contracted, 8 hours per week

The culinary supervisor will work with the Resident Director to ensure that all food, kitchens, and food handling equipment are safe and sanitary and in accordance with current health regulations. The culinary supervisor will be responsible for coordinating all efforts to prepare food in the premises, including any done by volunteer groups. The culinary supervisor will contact regular inspections and be responsible for making sure that all food, whether purchased or donated, is stored and handled properly and adheres to current nutrition guidelines.

QUALIFICATIONS FOR POSITION
High School diploma required. Some experience with food preparation and handling in a commercial setting required.

RECREATION AND ACTIVITIES

The Program Director, in conjunction with the Resident Director and Case Manager, shall be responsible for ensuring that the Discipleship Center has regular activities to help the residents. These activities shall include Christian 12 step meetings, Bible Studies, motivational talks, job training activities, community service projects, seminars, and other activities designed to keep the resident from idleness and to move the resident into self-sufficiency. Allowances should also be made from recreational activities. Program staff shall keep apprised of all recreational activities of the center, particularly in the immediate community, which would interest residents of the center.

VISITING POLICY AND WEEKEND PASSES

Residents shall be allowed to have visitors only during free time periods. Visitors must remain in common areas, and shall not be allowed in the residents' rooms. Business visitors (defined as professional persons assisting the resident with employment, legal, medical, financial, and spiritual issues), shall be allowed in the Center during free times and during the hours of 7:00 am – 5:00 pm Monday through Friday, unless an emergency exists. ConquestHouse employees, Board members, advisory committee members, and mentors may enter the building at any time. Other ConquestHouse volunteers may access the building during any non-curfew hour.

Residents may be allowed weekend passes to spend time away from the Center with a spouse. Weekend passes shall be from 7:30 p.m.

Friday through 10:00 p.m. Sunday, and shall be approved by the Resident Director, in consultation with the Resident's mentor, under the following conditions:

    a) Resident is legally married to his spouse.
    b) Spouse resides in the D.C. area.
    c) A determination is made that the resident's spending time with his spouse will improve his morale or hasten his progress in the Center.

A weekend pass excuses the resident from all center activities during the time the pass is issued for. Residents on a weekend pass are expected back at the Center by 10:00 pm Sunday.

EMERGENCY PASSES

Residents are allowed emergency passes. These passes are for a specific time period, during which the resident will be excused from all activities and curfews. Emergency passes will be issued in the following instances:

    a) A spouse or close family member or child dies
    b) A spouse or close family member or child is in the hospital or falls gravely ill.
    c) Medical emergency on the part of the resident

The Resident Director, at his discretion, shall issue emergency passes, provided he makes every effort to verify the reason for the issuance of the pass before it is issued.

STATEMENT OF FAITH

Each member of the Board of Directors, the Discipleship Committee, volunteers, staff, residents and mentors working directly with residents must sign the Statement of Faith below or provide one whose tenets are compatible with classical Christianity.

> The sole basis of my belief is the Bible, God's infallible written Word, the sixty-six books of the Old and New Testaments. I believe that it

was uniquely, verbally and fully inspired by the Holy Spirit and that it was written without error in the original manuscripts. It is the supreme and final authority in all matters on which it speaks.

I explicitly affirm my belief In basic Bible teachings, as follows:

1. There Is one true God, eternally existing in three persons -- Father, Son and Holy Spirit -- each of whom possesses equally all the attributes of Deity and the characteristics of personality.
2. Jesus Christ is God, the living Word, who became flesh through His miraculous conception by the Holy Spirit and His virgin birth. Hence, He is perfect Deity and true humanity united in one person forever.
3. He lived a sinless life and voluntarily atoned for the sins of men by dying on the cross as their substitute, thus satisfying divine justice and accomplishing salvation for all who trust In Him alone.
4. He rose from the dead in the same body, though glorified, in which He lived and died.
5. He ascended bodily into heaven and sat down at the right hand of God the Father. where He, the only mediator between God and man, continually makes intercession for His own.
6. Man was originally created in the image of God. He sinned by disobeying God, thus, he was alienated from his Creator. That historic fall brought all mankind under divine condemnation.
7. Man's nature is corrupted, and he is thus totally unable to please God. Every man is in need of regeneration and renewal by the Holy Spirit.
8. The salvation of man is wholly a work of God's free grace and is not the work, in whole or in part, of human works or goodness of religious ceremony. God imputes His righteousness to those who put their faith in Christ alone for their salvation, and thereby justifies them in His sight.
9. It is the privilege of all who are born again of the Spirit to be assured of their salvation from the very moment in which they trust Christ as their Savior. This assurance is not based upon any kind of human merit, but is produced by the witness of the Holy Spirit, who confirms in the believer the testimony of God in His written Word.
10. The Holy Spirit has come into the world to reveal and glorify

Christ and to apply the saving work of Christ to men. He convicts and draws sinners to Christ, imparts new life to them, continually indwells them from the moment of spiritual birth and seals them until the day of redemption. His fullness, power and control are appropriated in the believer's life by faith.

11. Every believer is called to live so in the power of the indwelling Spirit that he will not fulfill the lust of the flesh but will bear fruit to glorify God.
12. Jesus Christ is the Head of the Church, His Body, which is composed of all men, living and dead, who have been joined to Him through saving faith.
13. God admonishes His people to assemble together regularly for worship, for participation in ordinances, for edification through the Scriptures and for mutual encouragement.
14. At physical death the believer enters immediately into eternal, conscious fellowship with the Lord and awaits the resurrection of his body to everlasting glory and blessing.
15. At physical death the unbeliever enters immediately into eternal, conscious separation from the Lord and awaits the resurrection of his body to everlasting judgment and condemnation.
16. Jesus Christ will come again to the earth -- personally, visibly and bodily -- to consummate history and the eternal plan of God.
17. The Lord Jesus Christ commanded all believers to proclaim the Gospel throughout the world and to disciple men of every nation. The fulfillment of that Great Commission requires that all worldly and personal ambitions be subordinated to a total commitment to "Him who loved us and gave Himself for us."

Without mental reservation, I hereby subscribe to the above statements and pledge myself to help fulfill the Great Commission in our generation. depending upon the Holy Spirit to guide and empower me.

ENDNOTES

[1] Peter Baker, "Many Ex-Offenders Succeed After Release," *The Washington Post* (September 19, 1994):a01

[2] I say this only because of the potential problems that can exist because of females ministering to men who may have been devoid of female attention and interaction because of a lengthy incarceration. I would recommend that men minister to men and women minister to women. This avoids any complications and minimizes the temptation of or engaging in romantic or sexual relationships.

[3] "Faith-based Treatment gives addicts a new start", *ReligionToday* (Wednesday, July 22, 1998) at www.goshen.net

[4] An exception to this would be if the ex-offender is under orders by the court to perform certain family responsibilities, or if there is no one else available to assist with these responsibilities while the ex-offender is in study.

[5] H.R. 2137

[6] 42 USC 14071(d)

[7] Kenneth Copeland, Six Steps to Excellence in Ministry, @1987 Kenneth Copeland Publications

[8] Excerpted from a prison ministry training manual provided by Harvestime International. This manual is available on the World Wide Web at http://www.apeo.org/general/harvestime.